THE ECONOMICS OF THE PHARMACEUTICAL INDUSTRY

By the same author

ADVERTISING: ITS PLACE IN POLITICAL AND MANAGERIAL ECONOMICS

MANAGEMENT IN THE SOCIAL AND SAFETY SERVICES (*with N. C. Hunt)*

THE ECONOMICS OF THE PHARMACEUTICAL INDUSTRY

W. Duncan Reekie

First published 1975 by
THE MACMILLAN PRESS LTD
London and Basingstoke
Associated companies in New York
Dublin Melbourne Johannesburg and Madras

SBN 333 16690 6

Typeset in Great Britain by
PREFACE LIMITED
Salisbury, Wilts
and printed in Great Britain by
LEWIS REPRINTS
London and Tonbridge

For Basil

But know also, man has an inborn craving for medicine . . . the desire to take medicine is one feature which distinguishes man the animal, from his fellow creatures. It is really one of the most serious difficulties with which we have to contend.

William Osler, 1894

Contents

Acknowledgements

Past experience had forewarned me that in writing a book of this sort I would be indebted to literally dozens of individuals. This book would not have been possible without the assistance of the many executives of pharmaceutical firms who so willingly gave me their aid. In particular, I spent many hours scanning the library and records of the Association of the British Pharmaceutical Industry and the files of Intercontinental Medical Statistics Limited.

It would be remiss of me, however, not to mention two individuals by name. My interest in the industry was first aroused by Professor K. J. W. Alexander of the University of Strathclyde. His frequent counsel and interested advice proved an unfailing source of stimulus. Second, George Teeling-Smith, Director of the Office of Health Economics, read and commented on an early manuscript of this book. My own fascination with the pharmaceutical industry springs to no small degree from the infectious enthusiasm held for the subject by the Director of the OHE.

Finally, my thanks to my typists for transforming the manuscript into a readable whole.

The responsibility for the opinions expressed in the following chapters is exclusively my own.

W. DUNCAN REEKIE

1 Introduction

1 Definition

No two firms in the British pharmaceutical industry are alike. Their products range from fertilisers to antibiotics; from emulsion paints to tranquilisers. Many are subsidiaries of overseas parents, principally American, but also German, Swiss, Italian, Dutch and French. Only a few are quoted on the London Stock Exchange and one of these, ICI Ltd, has barely 2½ per cent of its turnover in pharmaceuticals. A precise definition of the 'pharmaceutical industry' is obviously necessary in order to isolate it conceptually from the wide variety of company types which participate in it.

Economists usually define an industry from one of two viewpoints; that of the producer or that of the consumer. From the producer's position, industry boundaries are indicated by the immobility of productive resources. If the same productive resources can be easily used to manufacture two or more distinct products, then the products come from the same industry. From the consumer's position, if two or more products are regarded as acceptable substitutes for one another then they are produced in the same industry.

The pharmaceutical industry as seen by the consumer is the group of firms manufacturing and distributing medicines in finished forms such as ointments, capsules, tablets and syrups. The industry as seen by the producer performs the following manufacturing and processing activities:

1. bulk manufacture of synthetic organic chemicals, such as vitamins, antihistamines, diuretics and sulphonamides. These, often complex, substances include many different classes of drugs;
2. bulk manufacture by fermentation, synthesis, or both of antibiotics, such as penicillin and streptomycin, which are normally

made by the culture of micro-organisms, followed by their extraction and purification;
3. preparation of sera and vaccines by micro-organism culture and the extraction and purification of the antibodies or antigens which are formed;
4. production from naturally occurring animal or vegetable sources of drugs such as insulin, hormones and morphines;
5. processing of bulk drugs into finished forms such as tablets, capsules and ointments.

Both definitions are necessary and are complementary. More specific restrictions will render them more precise. Products for veterinary use will not be included in the industry's product mix; nor will patent or proprietary medicines. Proprietary, or patent, medicines are products available for sale to the general public, and are frequently publicly advertised. The remaining products are known as ethical or prescription drugs.

The advertising of ethical drugs is restricted primarily to the medical profession. They are generally available to the public only if supplied by a pharmacist authorised by a doctor's prescription. A further important distinction between ethical and non-ethical or proprietary medicines is that the latter tend to have a low research content and a long product life. Ethical drugs, on the other hand, tend to be relatively short-lived and are usually products of a comparatively high degree of research effort.

It is with the ethical pharmaceutical industry that this book is concerned.

2 Origins and history

The saga of pharmacy began when man first applied herbs to relieve pain or dress wounds. From this initial step followed the blending of different herbs with each other or with chemicals, such as mercury or sublimed-sulphur. Between the twelfth and fourteenth centuries the British herbalist was adding drugs and spices of Arabian, and later, South American origin to his collection. These were introduced first by the Crusaders and later by various seafaring merchants. At this time, particularly in London, the grocery trade and the pepperers and spicers often overlapped. Their imports were frequently the same and so the functions of grocer and apothecary were often combined.

The increasing variety of unfamiliar drugs and the wider use of chemicals led to more specific skills being required in manufacture and

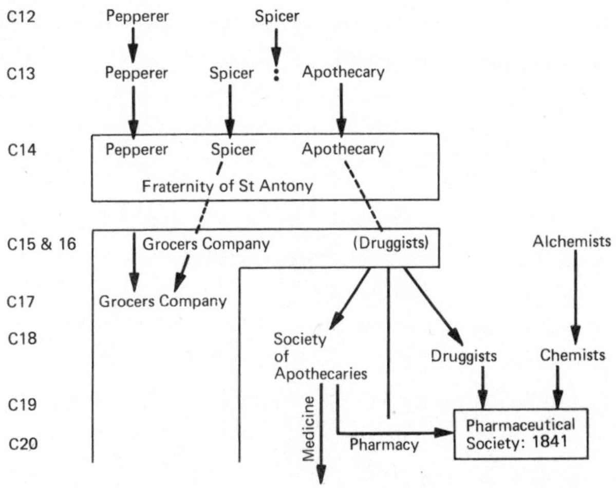

Fig. 1.1 Evolution of the London apothecary and pharmacist

Source: F. M. L. Poynter, *Evolution of Pharmacy in Britain* (Pitman, 1965).

blending. This made it increasingly difficult to combine the activities of grocer and apothecary and in 1617 the joint London Guild split up and the Society of Apothecaries was formed.

Over the next two centuries a gradual shift of emphasis from pharmacy to medicine occurred in the ranks of the apothecaries. This left a partial vacuum in the supply of drugs which was filled by retailing chemists and druggists. In 1841 the Pharmaceutical Society was formed which embraced the chemists, druggists and the remaining apothecaries with a predominant interest in pharmacy. Fig. 1.1 illustrates this development.

Many of these chemists and druggists developed into wholesalers and ultimately into manufacturers. Some of today's familiar names in the pharmaceutical industry developed from such origins. For example the retail chemists and druggists of the nineteenth century, Allen, Hanburys and Barry, is today's Allen and Hanbury Ltd.

Increasing complexity of manufacture was one factor in the trend away from back-shop to factory production. The hand-rolled pill gave way to the compressed tablet. Processes such as varnishing, gilding or silvering pills 'to disguise unpleasant odours or taste ... were superseded by the introduction of sugar and pearl coatings which were difficult to perform on a dispensing scale with the result that these coated pills, and indeed most pills, passed into the hands of the large scale manufacturer'.[1]

The most important factor accelerating this trend was the advent of chemotherapy which transferred many of the functions of the pharmacist to the chemist, pharmacologist and clinician. The beginnings of chemotherapy are associated with the name of Paul Ehrlich (1854–1915). Ehrlich built on Robert Koch's observations that certain aniline dyes could kill bacteria. Ehrlich realised that if these dyes could attach themselves to diseased bacteria without harming whole body tissues or cells then he would have made a tremendous contribution to medical science. His search for the 'Magic Bullet', a drug which would seek out its own target, was not short.

Eventually, in 1904, his researches produced salvarsan, a 'Magic Bullet' which kills cellular organisms connected with syphilis.

Despite this promising start, a quarter of a century had to pass before the next major pharmaceutical discovery. Calder has pointed out that before 1935 the physician had only six specific medicines in his armoury; that is, medicines 'capable of attacking causes'. The six were vitamin therapy, quinine, digitalis, ipecacuanha, mercury and salvarsan. 'Only one, Ehrlich's salvarsan, was a truly modern preparation'.[2]

In 1935 what is now called the 'therapeutic revolution' was launched. Dr Gerhard Domagk discovered the antimicrobial qualities of 'Prontosil', a red dye. A year or two later, in France, it was established that it was an active constituent of the dye, sulphonilamide, which was active therapeutically. Attempts to improve the efficacy of 'Prontosil' resulted in the production of May & Baker Ltd's M & B 693 in 1938.

Penicillin, although discovered by Fleming in 1928, became first available for practical purposes after 1940. Streptomycin, a drug effective against tuberculosis was discovered by Waksman in 1943, and the first of the broad-spectrum antibiotics (chloramphenicol) was introduced in 1949. Tetracycline, 1953, was the first antibiotic to be produced where its chemical formula was known prior to the drug itself.[4]

By 1950 the therapeutic revolution was well and truly under way. Corticosteriods, antihistamines, antidepressants, diuretics and many other preparations helping to alleviate human ailments were discovered, developed and are now being produced by the drug industry. Fig. 1.2 clearly illustrates the path of the therapeutic revolution and the spectacular increase in the number of known, important drugs which began with the discovery of Prontosil. Table 1.1, showing pharmaceutical patent activity in London from 1900, provides a similar

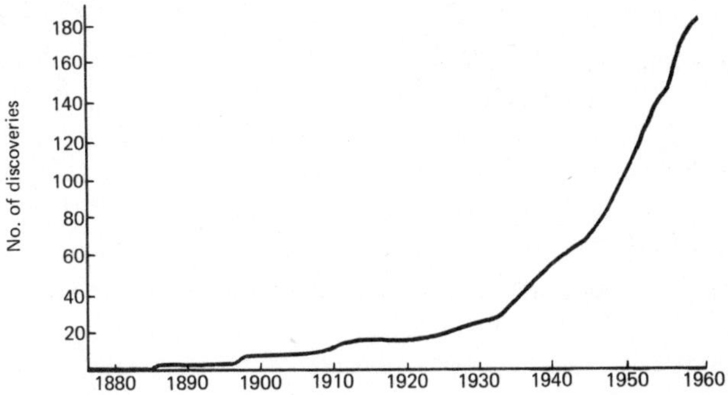

Fig.1.2 Cumulative principal pharmaceutical discoveries 1875–1960

Source: Sub-Committee on Anti-Trust, United States Senate, 87th Congress, 1st Session, No. 448, 1962.

picture. A tremendous upsurge of patenting activity occurs after 1935, most noticeably, in fact, after 1944. By the end of the 1951–2 period more than twice the number of patents had been taken out in the eight years up to 1944 than had been taken out in the remainder of the

Table 1.1 Patent acceptances, 1900–66, London Patent Office

Period	*Patents*	*'Five-yearly'*	*Period*	*Patents*	*'Five-yearly'*
1900–10	161	161	1951–52	380	1,563
1910–14	73	73	1952–53	352	
1916–20	16	16	1953–54	474	
1921–25	47	47	1954–55	528	
1926–30	138		1955–56	643	
1931–32	63	201	1956–57	723	2,720
1932–33	43		1957–58	932	
1933–34	29		1958–59	553	
1934–35	70	142	1959–60	793	
1935–37	78		1960	710	
1937–38	131		1960–61	956	3,944
1939–40	148		1961–62	1,018	
1940–41	139		1962–63	755	
1941–44	252		1963	839	
1944–46	284	536	1963–64	672	
1946–48	311		1964	776	
1948–49	295		1964–65	722	
1949–50	384		1965–66	867	
1950–51	193		1966	938	6,587

Source: W. D. Reekie, Patent Data as a Guide to Industrial Activity, *Research Policy*, 2 (1973), p. 250.

century. This rapid spurt does not appear to have been an isolated instance. More than double the number of patents had been taken out between 1958–9 and 1966 than in the first fifty-eight years of the century. In other words exponential growth is present with little sign yet of a levelling off.

In Fig. 1.3 the function recording pharmaceutical patenting activity is displaying classic exponential growth and in 1966 was still

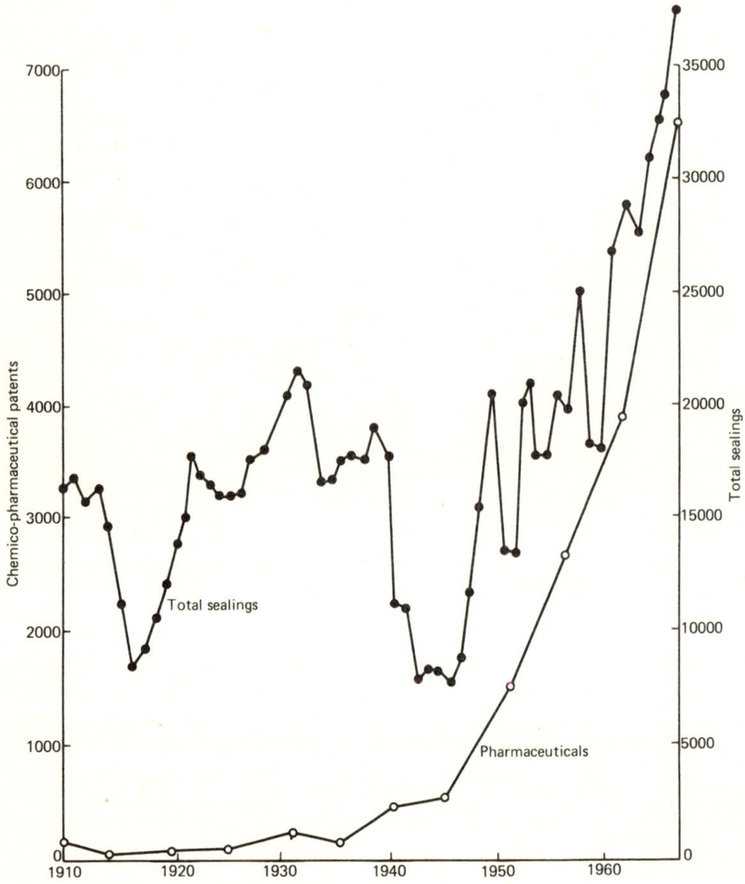

Fig. 1.3 Chemico-pharmaceutical patents in five-yearly periods and total annual patent sealings, 1910–1966

Source: W. D. Reekie, 'Patent Data as a Guide to Industrial Activity', *Research Policy*, 2 (1973) p. 249.

showing no sign of having reached a 'ceiling' and reverting to the more familiar S-shaped logistic curve. Superimposed on Fig. 1.3 is a function showing the annual pattern of total patent sealings at the London Patent Office since 1910. This comparison emphasises that pharmaceutical inventive activity has expanded, not merely absolutely, but also relatively to all other patented inventions.

3 Recent growth

The chemists and druggists who began to manufacture in the nineteenth century had to adopt many new techniques after the chemotherapeutic revolution. Knowledge of technologies associated with chemical processing and dyestuffs expertise and with fermentation was essential. Simultaneously entry into pharmaceuticals by firms engaged in industries which already utilised these techniques was occurring – for example ICI Dyestuffs Division and Distillers Co. Ltd, respectively. This process of industrial expansion and technological advance was replicated overseas.

In Britain this coincided with an increasing awareness and demand for the benefits of good health, which was formalised by the establishment in 1948 of the National Health Service. The combination resulted in a tremendous expansion in the output of the industry, by existing members, by entrants from other industries and by immigrant subsidiaries bringing with them discoveries and products unique to themselves.

The impact of the world-wide increase in drug discoveries is mirrored in the record of entry by overseas companies into the UK market. The Association of the British Pharmaceutical Industry, whose members supply the NHS with almost all of its drug purchases, has around fifty foreign-owned member companies. Six of these are old-established companies in the UK with dates of entry of 1920 or earlier. A further nine entered between 1920 and 1935. The remainder all entered the British market as subsidiaries subsequent to the discovery of Prontosil in 1935.

These companies did not gain a foothold in the UK market because they attempted to produce existing drugs at a lower price, they succeeded because they were offering newly discovered unique products. This process of discovery and breaking into foreign markets is still going on. Fourteen companies have set up subsidiaries here since 1960, including five after 1966. Similarly Beecham, a UK firm with a number of recent major discoveries to its credit, has set up five overseas manufacturing subsidiaries since 1963.

A more comprehensive picture of the impact of the post-1935 wave of discoveries is given in Table 1.2 which illustrates how the industry's output rose by almost 400 per cent (at current prices) between 1935 and 1948. Between 1950 and 1965 it rose a further 320 per cent. Table 1.3 provides a more recent picture of the industry's place in the economy.

This compares the relative growth and size of output levels of the pharmaceutical chemicals and preparations industry with the chemicals industry as a whole and with total manufacturing industry over the period 1963–72. As can be seen, the drug industry with an annual growth rate of 9.7 per cent is expanding faster than manufacturing industry as a whole. It is also growing more rapidly than the total chemicals industry of which it is a member. This again reflects the twin impacts of a high innovation rate on supply and the increasing social awareness of good health on demand. The table also illustrates the comparative size of the industry. In 1970 it accounted for less than

Table 1.2 Output of the British pharmaceutical industry, 1924–65

Date	*Output* £m*	*Output* £m*	*Employees**	*Date*	*Output £m*	*Employees*
1924	15.2			1954	116.5	62,000
1934	16.9			1955	129.6	62,000
1935	19.0			1956	134.7	64,000
1937	21.0			1957	144.4	64,000
1946	60.2			1958	158.5	66,000
1948	73.0			1959	176.0	67,000
1949	–	76.0	42,000	1960	192.2	73,000
1950	–	n.a.	n.a.	1961	211.3	73,000
1951	–	110.0	48,000	1962	212.3	74,000
1952	–	104.8	49,000	1963	223.6	77,000
1953	–	106.6	55,000	1964	245.3	74,000
–	–	–	–	1965	280.3	–

*Output figures for pre- and post-1948/9 are not directly comparable. Pre-1949 figures include all sales by establishments whose main products were pharmaceutical preparations and excludes sales of such preparations by establishments whose main product was not pharmaceutical preparations. Post-1948 figures include veterinary products and inter-establishment sales. Both sets include non-prescription medicines.

Employee statistics include persons engaged in the manufacture of toilet preparations and perfumes.

Source: British Information Service, 'The British Pharmaceutical Industry'.

Table 1.3 Size and growth of the industry, 1963–72

		Total manufacturing industry	*Total chemical industry*	*Pharmaceutical chemicals & preparations*
(1)	*Index of production*			
	1963	100	100	100
	1964	109	110	111
	1965	112	117	126
	1966	114	123	145
	1967	114	130	156
	1968	121	140	167
	1969	126	149	189
	1970	127	158	208
	1971	127	160	219
	1972	130	169	230
	1973	134	178	242
(2)	*Annual growth rate*			
	1963–72	3.0%	6.0%	9.7%
	1971–72	2.8%	5.6%	5.0%
(3)	*Gross output*	£m	£m	£m
	1963	27826.1	2163.6	237.2
	1968	39658.0	3247.4	347.2
	1970	46304.8	3777.9	432.8

Source: Department of Trade and Industry.

1 per cent by value of manufacturing industry gross output, and 11 per cent of chemical industry output.

4 Benefits produced by the industry

Measuring the benefits produced for society by the industry raises a number of complications beyond the scope of this discussion. The benefits can be social, economic or a mixture of both. They may well be the resultants of costs other than those required to purchase the manufacture of existing drugs or the discovery of new ones. Any attempt to measure the benefits is hampered in two main ways.

Firstly, there is the classic welfare economics situation in that not all the relevant costs and benefits may be apparent in the workings of the market as economists normally see it. Secondly, having identified the benefits, it may be impossible to ascertain what proportion of them result from the pharmaceutical industry's operations.

The all-embracing benefit produced by the industry is the improvement of the health of the community. However, identification of that part of improved health due to the drug industry's operations is almost impossible. Improved health is the result not only of advances in medicines; it is also a consequence of higher standards of hygiene, of nutrition, of increased knowledge in fields such as physiology, of improved surgical techniques and many other factors.

Improved health is usually measured by comparative mortality and/or morbidity statistics. Unfortunately such statistics are not easily convertible into meaningful economic measures. Rare attempts have been made to apply cost-benefit analysis techniques to such statistics. One study by Weisbrod lists the economic losses to society of poor health or, conversely, the economic gains of improved health. These include:

1. Premature death causing the loss of a present or future producer.
2. Loss of production during sickness.
3. Productivity and/or future disease-resistance may be lowered after return to work.
4. Disruption of production of absentee's fellow-workers (due to having to 'fill in' etc.) may mean society's economic loss is greater than the individual's.
5. Economic costs of detection, treatment and rehabilitation of patients.[5]

To obtain an accurate economic assessment of the gains of improved health, such benefits would have to be computed for each individual and subsequently discounted to obtain the present value of the future stream of benefits. The difficulties associated with such a task possibly explain why the problem has been so infrequently approached empirically.

Even were such exercises carried out, it still seems unlikely that the contribution made by any one factor, such as the drug industry, would be able to be assessed. The causes of non-economic benefits would be equally difficult to isolate and such benefits themselves would be non-quantifiable. For example, relief from suffering for the patient and the simultaneous reduction in distress for the patient's relatives and dependants.

In a few disease areas, however, it is possible to obtain a picture of the welfare contribution of the industry to society. This occurs where the incidence or killing power of the disease has abruptly declined after a relevant pharmaceutical breakthrough. Tables 1.4 and 1.5 illustrate this. They show some of the disease areas where improved health

Table 1.4 Deaths from tuberculosis, 1920–60

Year	*Deaths per 100,000 of population*	*% decrease*
1920	113.1	–
1930	71.1	37
1940	45.9	35.4
1950	22.5	51.1
1960	5.9	73.8

Source: The Registrar General's *Statistical Review.*

benefits are due largely to the industry's introduction, manufacture and distribution of new medicines.

Table 1.4 indicates how tuberculosis was gradually becoming less important as a killing disease due to improved social and medical conditions. This trend was dramatically accelerated between 1940 and 1950 due to the discovery of streptomycin and the other anti-tubercular drugs. In Table 1.5 deaths from pneumonia and influenza show a similar but less obvious trend following the discovery of the sulphonamides, penicillin and other antibiotics. The impact of the drugs on mortality was probably greater than is apparent from a first glance at the tables. It may be that the effects of rising standards of hygiene and of life on the mortality rates were beginning to suffer from diminishing returns by the 1940s. If this is so, the contribution of pharmaceuticals would be greater than the simple comparison of mortality rates suggests.

Mortality rates among children in this country have declined continuously since the mid-nineteenth century (apart from some of the war years when mortality rates were exceptionally high). There are many contributory factors, including public health measures and

Table 1.5 Deaths from pneumonia* and influenza

Year	*Deaths per 100,000 of population*	*% decrease*
1920	207.3	–
1930	102.5	51
1940	70.3	30.5
1950	31.3	55.1
1960	36.6	no decrease

*This excludes pneumonia of the newborn.

Source: The Registrar General's *Statistical Review.*

improved social and economic conditions. In the late 1930s the rate of improvement in mortality rates accelerated rapidly. Coincidental with the change was the introduction of new medicines and vaccines which were capable of preventing or curing many diseases which had hitherto been fatal. One study by the Office of Health Economics (OHE) attempted to quantify the contribution of these revolutionary advances in medicine in preventing premature mortality among children aged 1–14.

The calculation made by the OHE rests on the assumption that, if there had not been this rapid expansion in the effectiveness of medical intervention in the natural history of diseases, then mortality rates in the last thirty years would only have declined at the same rate as they had done between 1901 and 1935. Fig. 1.4 illustrates the disparity between actual mortality rates over the past thirty years and projected mortality rates on the basis of the 1901–35 trend. The shaded area represents what may be considered as 'lives saved' by the accelerated reduction in mortality.

In 1968, the total number of deaths among 1–14 year olds was 496

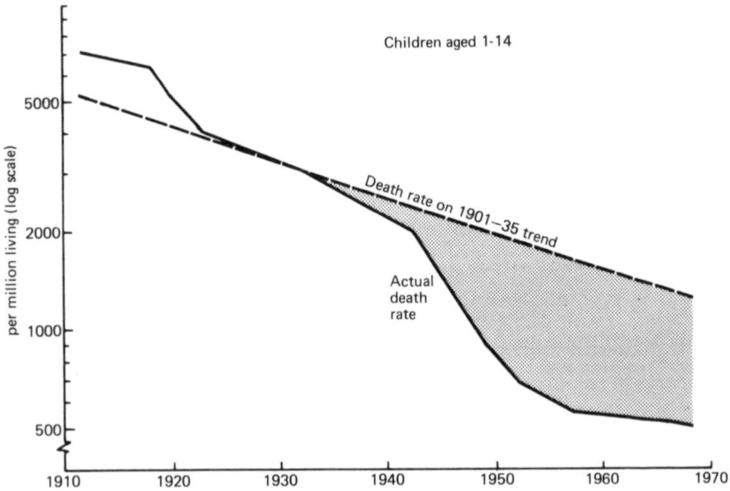

Fig. 1.4 Death rate per million living, England and Wales 1911/15–1968. 5-yearly averages 1911/15–1961/5; annual rates 1966–8.

Source: Office of Health Economics.

per million living, or 5235 in absolute numbers. Projected deaths on the 1901–35 trend would have been 1207 per million living, or 12,750 in absolute numbers. Thus in 1968 there were 7500 less childhood deaths than there would otherwise have been. Over half of the improvement can be attributed to the near eradication of deaths from five diseases, pneumonia, tuberculosis, diphtheria, measles and whooping cough. In 1931–5 these were responsible for a total of 1570 deaths a year among every million children living. In 1968, this total had been reduced to 51 per million living, of which 46 were due to pneumonia. By comparing actual with projected mortality rates, an estimate can be made of the total number of lives saved since 1935.

Table 1.6 indicates that there were in total about 227,000 persons alive in 1968 who would have died in childhood had the abrupt change in the rate of decline of mortality rates not taken place.

A further obvious contribution to health is the production of insulin, and more recently the discovery and production of anti-diabetic drugs such as the sulphonylureas. Diabetes sufferers have not been cured by these medicines but they do allow them to lead virtually normal lives. In the past severe cases of diabetes headed towards certain death. This is no longer the case. Compared with the 1920s, some 2000 deaths per year have been averted because of insulin.[6] In less severe cases the rigid and unpleasant diet of the diabetic is a thing of the past.

The discovery of the first of the tranquillisers in 1952 and of the anti-depressants in 1960 led to the commencement of psycho-pharmacology. The use of psychotherapeutic drugs was a major cause, in 1956, of the first-ever annual decrease in the number of occupied hospital beds due to mental illness. From 151,000 in-patients in 1956, the mental illness hospital population fell to 125,000 in 1966 and 103,600 in 1971.[7]

Decreased use of mental hospital beds was paralleled in other diseases. Improving drug therapy enabled the general practitioner to assume functions previously undertaken by the hospital consultant. For example, Taylor, as early as 1954, said that 'today the practitioner in the gloomiest slum practice can treat pneumonia more effectively than the most eminent specialist was able to do before the war'.[8] This statement is now true of many diseases. Since GP treatment is considerably cheaper per patient than is residence in hospital, this is a further important benefit produced by the industry. (A prescription costs on average, about 82p in total, including chemist's remuneration. If this can prevent hospitalisation, it will mean a saving of over £79 a week, the cost for one patient in the average general hospital.)

Table 1.6 Numbers and ages of persons alive in 1968 who would have died in childhood had mortality rates continued on the 1901–35 trend

	1–4	*5–9*	*10–14*	*15–19*	*20–24*	*25–29*	*30–34*	*35–39*	*40–44*	*Total*
Age when saved										
1–4	8,900	17,200	20,200	25,300	13,200	10,500	7,600			102,900
5–9		9,100	14,600	16,700	18,600	12,800	4,500	2,200		78,500
10–14			5,100	10,000	11,200	9,300	7,100	1,900	1,700	46,300
Totals	8,900	26,300	39,900	52,000	43,000	32,600	19,200	4,100	1,700	227,700
Died later*				100	230	315	170	85	40	940

*This represents the number of persons (out of the 227,700 whose deaths were prevented in childhood) who would, on the basis of actual mortality rates, have died after the age of 14.

Source: OHE.

In summary, the benefits produced by the drug industry are almost impossible to isolate, are frequently immeasureable and usually unmeasured. However, this brief review may have gone a little way to show the colossal contribution which the industry has made to society. For 'there can be little doubt of the need to remind us of what has been achieved for our benefit'.[9]

5 The costs of the pharmaceutical industry

The costs of obtaining the above benefits are more easily measured. The direct monetary cost of the industry to the nation is the bill presented by the industry to its monopsonistic* customer, the NHS. The individual consumers of drugs in Britain are supplied with them, free, or at a flat rate charge, direct from hospital or by means of a doctor's prescription from a retail chemist. The prescription charge to the patient bears no relation to the cost of the medicine and is remitted ultimately to the NHS, not to the company responsible for the drug.

To this can be added a number of ancillary costs such as wholesale distributors' margins, retail chemists' margins, professional pharmacists' fees and retailers' container allowances. The aggregation of these varying costs for the Department of Health and Social Security and the Scottish Home and Health Department for drug consumption through hospitals, local authorities and retail pharmacists give the total NHS expenditure on pharmaceutical services in the United Kingdom.

Table 1.7 shows how on this gross basis total expenditure by the NHS, plus payments by patients, on pharmaceutical services in the United Kingdom in 1971 was £245 million. At 10.3 per cent of total expenditures on all NHS services, this proportion has remained almost unchanged for twenty years. Of the £245 million, manufacturers' sales accounted for £153 million, while wholesalers' and pharmacists' margins and dispensing fees totalled £90 million.

The number and average cost of prescriptions is indicated in Table 1.8. Prescription charges were first introduced in June 1951 at 1*s* per form. They were raised in December 1956 to 1*s* per item, and again in March 1961 to 2*s* per item. The Labour government abolished them in February 1965, and reimposed them in June 1968 at 2*s* 6*d* per item. In April 1971, they were raised to 20p per item.

*A technical term meaning a single or large customer who can affect price by threatening to withdraw custom.

Table 1.7 NHS total expenditure and expenditure on pharmaceutical services, United Kingdom

Year	*Total NHS £m*	*Pharmaceutical £m*	*% NHS*	*% National income*
1950	477	40	8.4	0.50
1951	500	52	10.4	0.44
1952	523	55	10.5	0.43
1953	548	54	9.9	0.39
1954	567	57	10.1	0.39
1955	607	60	9.9	0.39
1956	662	70	10.6	0.42
1957	721	74	10.3	0.41
1958	764	80	10.5	0.43
1959	828	88	10.6	0.45
1960	902	97	10.8	0.46
1961	981	100	10.2	0.45
1962	1025	103	10.0	0.44
1963	1092	115	10.5	0.46
1964	1186	126	10.6	0.47
1965	1308	151	11.5	0.53
1966	1434	166	11.6	0.55
1967	1594	177	11.1	0.56
1968	1741	184	10.6	0.55
1969	1886	198	10.5	0.56
1970	2158	220	10.2	0.57
1969	1823*	198	10.9	0.56
1970	2083*	220	10.6	0.57
1971	2369*	245	10.3	0.57
1972	2732	277	10.1	0.58

*Change in definition of NHS from 1969 onwards. Certain local authority services transferred from NHS to Social Services.

Source: Annual Abstract of Statistics, National Income and Expenditure. NHS expenditure includes local authority expenditure and payments by patients. 'Pharmaceutical services' include surgery dispensing, distribution costs and chemists' dispensing payments, but exclude drugs dispensed in hospitals.

Table 1.8 NHS prescriptions, number and average cost, England & Wales

Year	*Prescription charge*	*Number of prescriptions (million)*	*Average total cost per prescription (p)*	*Year*	*Prescription charge*	*Number of prescriptions (million)*	*Average total cost per prescription (p)*
1949		202.0	15				
1950	nil	217.1	16	1960	1*s* per item	218.7	36
1951	nil	227.7	18	1961	2*s* per item from March	205.0	41
1952	1*s* per form from June	216.0	20	1962	2*s* per item	196.6	44
1953	1*s* per form	219.8	20	1963	2*s* per item	205.5	47
1954	1*s* per form	218.7	21	1964	2*s* per item	209.4	50
1955	1*s* per form	226.1	22	1965	Abolished in February	244.3	52
1956	1*s* per item from December	228.9	25	1966	nil	262.0	53
1957	1*s* per item	207.2	29	1967	nil	271.2	54
1958	1*s* per item	203.4	32	1968	2*s* 6*d* per item from June	267.4	57
1959	1*s* per item	214.0	34	1969	2*s* 6*d* per item	264.2	62
				1970	2*s* 6*d* per item	266.6	67
				1971	20*p* per item from April	266.5	76
				1972	20*p* per item	275.8	82
				1973	20*p* per item	284.1	88

Source: Department of Health and Social Security, *Annual Reports.*

As can be seen, charges have some effect on prescription numbers. Falls were recorded in 1952, 1957, 1961, 1968/9 and 1971, the years of increased charges. Rises were recorded in almost all other years, including a 35 million rise in 1965, the year of abolition. However, charges also raise the average cost of a prescription because doctors tend to prescribe in larger quantities when the patient has to make a payment.*

*This discussion ignores those who are exempt from payment on grounds, for example, of low income, age, pregnancy or because they are mothers of babies under 12 months. Thus, of 256 million prescriptions dispensed in England in 1972, 150 million were dispensed without charge to the patient; these figures in turn include prescriptions dispensed for holders of a prepayment, or 'season ticket', certificate, which costs £2 for a six-month certificate, £3.50 for a twelve-month certificate. (In total, 223,000 such certificates were issued in 1972.)

2 Structure and Morphology

1 Market concentration and firm size

Although there are some 120 firms engaged in the manufacture and distribution of ethical drugs in Britain, it was estimated by the Sainsbury Committee that 60 of these firms account for more than 95 per cent of all sales to the NHS while 53 supply approximately 90 per cent. There is no reason to believe that the share these companies hold of British exports of ethicals is much, if at all different from their share of the NHS market.

Table 2.1 gives the size distribution of firms by sales to both home and export markets for the 53 companies. There is considerable variation in size of company. There is a large 'tail' of some 60 companies controlling approximately 10 per cent of the market. Twenty-three companies supply 7.9 per cent of the remainder of the market, but at the upper concentration levels 44 per cent of this remainder is controlled by only six companies, 61 per cent by only eleven companies.

A more recent survey by the National Economic Development Office (NEDO) provides an indication of the distribution of net assets, as well as sales, amongst firms of different sizes (Table 2.2).

Two complementary factors of particular importance emerge from these tables. The first is the large number of small producers which exist side by side with large and medium scale firms. Secondly, this is at least partly explained by the absence of any obvious benefits proceeding from economies of scale in the industry. The 1958 Census of Production revealed that 4.9 per cent of industry output is produced in the smallest size of establishment by 4.9 per cent of industry

Table 2.1 Analysis of companies by sales of ethical pharmaceuticals, 1965

Sales £m	*No. companies*	*% total*
less than 1	23	7.9
1–2.1/2	10	10.5
2.1/2–5	9	20.6
5–7.1/2	5	17.0
7.1/2–10	3	16.8
over £10	3	27.2
Totals	53	100.0

Source: Report of the Committee of Inquiry into the Relationship of the Pharmaceutical Industry with the National Health Service, Cmnd 3410, 1967 (The Sainsbury Report) pp. 100–1.

employees; while in establishments of over 500 employees 54 per cent of the output is produced by 56 per cent of industry employees.

A not dissimilar picture is presented by the 1968 Census. It appears there that net output per head in the chemical industry as a whole varies little by size of establishment. In the pharmaceutical industry, however, there is a noticeable variation, with establishments in the 500–999 employee size range having, on average, the highest net output per head. In very large drug firms this lower productivity is probably the result of the existence of a number of large R & D establishments.

While this is partly due to the small minimum size required for efficient operation of manufacturing processes, it is also a result of the

Table 2.2 Distribution of net assets and sales amongst 110 pharmaceutical companies, 1969

	% of total net assets and sales in companies ranged by net assets						
	Total £m	*Largest 20*	*2nd 20*	*3rd 20*	*4th 20*	*5th 20*	*Remaining 10*
Net assets	266	81.6	13.4	3.0	1.4	0.5	0.1
Sales	447	69.2	20.2	6.2	2.9	1.1	0.4

Source: Focus on Pharmaceuticals, National Economic Development Office, 1972 p. 16.

wide variety of products turned out by the industry. A small plant concentrating on only one or a few products can compete effectively with a larger factory turning out a wider range.

2 The sub-market concept

Up to this juncture, the term pharmaceutical industry has been used to refer to that group of firms which use specified manufacturing techniques to produce ethical drugs. Within the total market, however, there are a number of sub-markets, the medicines produced to satisfy the demand in any one sub-market being of little or no value to satisfy the demand in the others. Between the sub-markets there is generally a very low cross-elasticity of demand, although cross-elasticity of supply may well be quite high if the same producer can supply the needs of a variety of differing sub-markets. This is not a contradictory concept since the same manufacturing techniques can frequently be used to produce drugs with entirely different pharmacological functions.

Within each sub-market or therapeutic grouping, there will be a number of medicines available to the patient, each of which will be appropriate to a greater or lesser degree to be used as a treatment for the patient's ailment. The drugs in other therapeutic groupings, on the other hand, will not possess the necessary medicinal qualities required of substitutes. There is consequently much scope for competition within the various sub-markets but for very little between them.

Within the sub-markets, the picture of market structure is somewhat altered, as Table 2.3 indicates. The number of companies operating in any one sub-market ranges from one to 36 with modal values of ten and seventeen and a mean of thirteen. The proportion of any one sub-market held by its leading company ranges from 18.9 per cent to 100 per cent with a mode of around 36 per cent and a mean of 42.5 per cent.

Companies in the industry are not, therefore, faced with a highly fragmented market with 68 participants where no one firm has a share higher than 8.2 per cent but are rather operating in a series of markets with varying degrees of oligopolistic concentration.

3 Ownership patterns

Although the three leading companies which accounted for 27.2 per cent of the industry's output were all three British-owned, British-

Table 2.3 Participation in, and control of therapeutic sub-markets, 1966

Market	*No. of firms participating*	*% of market held by leading company*
Total market	68	8.2
Analgesics	21	27.1
Anaesthetics	7	38.4
Antacids	16	36.0
Antihelminthics	4	36.4
Anti-inflammatory agents	17	41.3
Antibacterials and antiseptics	11	51.2
Antibiotics	24	23.8
Anticoagulants	3	89.4
Anticonvulsants	17	24.7
Antidiarrhoeals	12	24.6
Antihistamines	14	29.4
Antinauseants	7	59.5
Anti-obesity preparations	10	24.9
Antispasmodics and anticholinergics	15	30.1
Bile therapy	5	50.6
Biologicals and allergens	7	38.5
Bronchial dilators and asthma remedies	19	34.7
Cardiovascular preparations	32	42.1
Gynaecological preparations	14	48.7
Contraceptives	9	31.5
Cough and cold preparations	36	19.3
Dermatological preparations	35	18.9
Diabetic therapy	9	29.8
Diagnostic agents	1	100.0
Diuretics	11	41.6
Enzymes and digestives	11	44.8
Haematinics	17	26.9
Haemorrhoidal preparations	10	47.9
Haemostats	7	51.0
Hormones	34	25.5
Laxatives	10	36.0
Lipotropics and cholesterol reducers	3	84.3
Muscle relaxants	6	52.9
Oxytocins	3	41.6
Parasympathetic agents	1	100.0
Psychotropics	17	36.4
Sedatives and hypnotics	16	29.2
Sulphonamides	12	21.3
TB preparations	10	34.3
Thyroid therapy	2	58.6
Vitamins & nutrients	17	20.8

Source: Intercontinental Medical Statistics.

Table 2.4 Sales of ethical drugs by nationality of company ownership, 1966

Nationality of Parent	*Number of companies*	*Sales £m*	*% sales*
British	22	64.3	40.0
USA	17	64.2	40.0
Swiss	5	14.9	9.25
Other European	9	17.4	10.8
Total	53	160.8	100.0

Source: Sainsbury, op. cit., pp. 100–1.

owned companies as a whole accounted for only 40 per cent of sales, the remaining 60 per cent having been produced by foreign-owned subsidiaries operating in Britain. Table 2.4 illustrates the share of the market controlled by the various nationalities of ultimate ownership.

Thirteen of the British companies had sales of less than £1m per annum while five of the American, two of the Swiss and one other European firm all had sales of over £5m per annum. Thus, if it were not for the predominance of the three leading companies, British control of the output of the industry would be very weak indeed.

The presence or absence of such control need not, in itself, be either a good or a bad thing from the standpoint of the economy. Since the output of the industry is based on the results of a continuous research and development (R & D) effort and since the bulk of the discoveries have been made since 1940, it is safe to deduce that a considerable proportion of all drugs manufactured will either be patented or will only recently have lost patent cover. This is borne out by the available evidence. Sainsbury discovered that 71.8 per cent by value of drugs supplied to the NHS in 1965 were patented. It is probable that most of the remaining 28.2 per cent had also at one time been subject to patent.

British discoveries, however, amounted to only 4.8 per cent of total drug discoveries between 1941 and 1963. The USA accounted for over 61 per cent, Switzerland for 7.9 per cent and Germany and France together for 9.2 per cent of discoveries. Table 2.5 gives an international analysis of major discoveries. Each of the countries listed, with the sole exception of Italy with one discovery to its credit, provides patent protection for pharmaceutical discoveries. This does not mean that all of the remaining 586 discoveries were patented but the fact remains that 71.8 per cent of drugs supplied to the NHS in 1965 were, or had

Table 2.5 Country of origin of discovery of single chemical entities, 1941–63

Country	*Number of drugs*	*% of total*
USA	355	61.1
Switzerland	44	7.9
Germany	32	5.7
UK	27	4.8
France	21	3.5
Holland	8	1.3
Denmark	6	1.0
Mexico	6	1.2
Sweden	5	0.8
Belgium	3	0.5
Japan	3	0.5
Austria	3	0.5
Argentina	1	0.2
Australia	1	0.2
Czechoslovakia	1	0.2
Italy	1	0.2
Compound previously known	14	2.3
Source not reported	46	8.1
Total	577	
'Shared credit'	10	
Totals	587	100.0

Source: Paul de Haen, 'Compilation of New Drugs: 1941–63', *American Professional Pharmicist*, 1964.

been, subject to patent protection; and that of all the major discoveries made since 1941, Britain was responsible for only 4.8 per cent and that 95 per cent of the remainder were discovered in national atmospheres likely to result in patenting.

Similar evidence is provided by Figs. 2.1 and 2.2. Moreover, it indicates that in the last few years the trend has been for the British-controlled share of pharmaceutical patenting to decline relative to the rest of the world.

Fig. 2.1 gives an analysis of all pharmaceutical patent acceptances between 1900 and 1966 analysed by nationality of patentee and by Patent Office publication period. (The lengths of these periods vary and so do the months of the year in which they commence and end.) Fig. 2.2 presents the same data in simplified form in approximately equal five-yearly periods.

Consumers of pharmaceuticals have several options open to them in

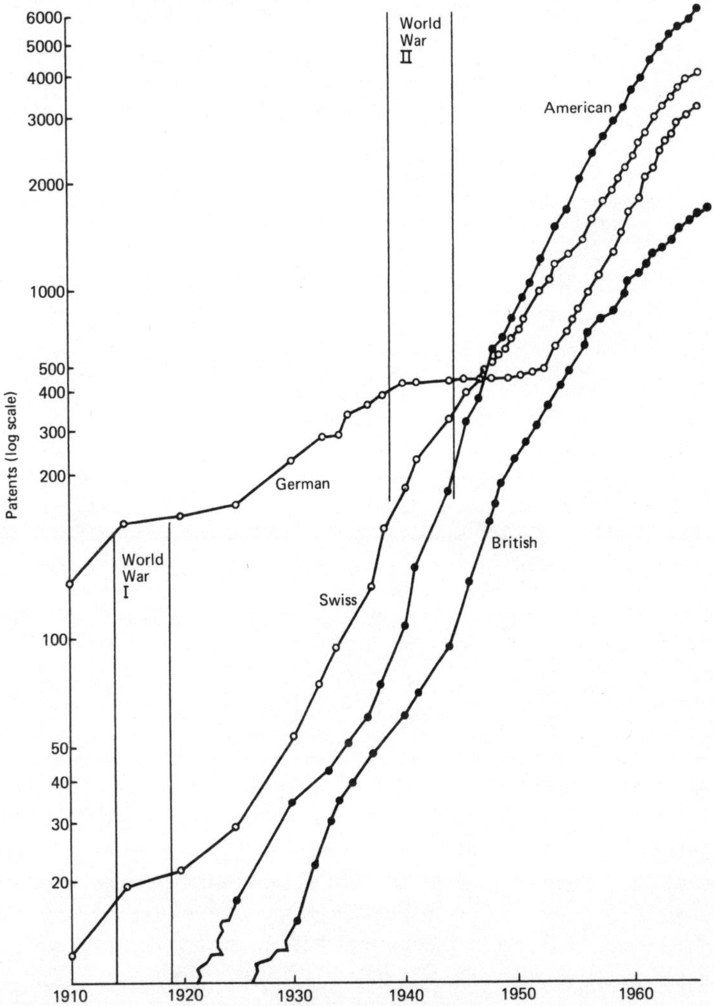

Fig. 2.1 Cumulative pharmaceutical patents, 1910–66, by nationality of patentee

Source: W. D. Reekie, 'Patent Data as Guide to Inventive Activity', *Research Policy*, 2 (1973) p. 254.

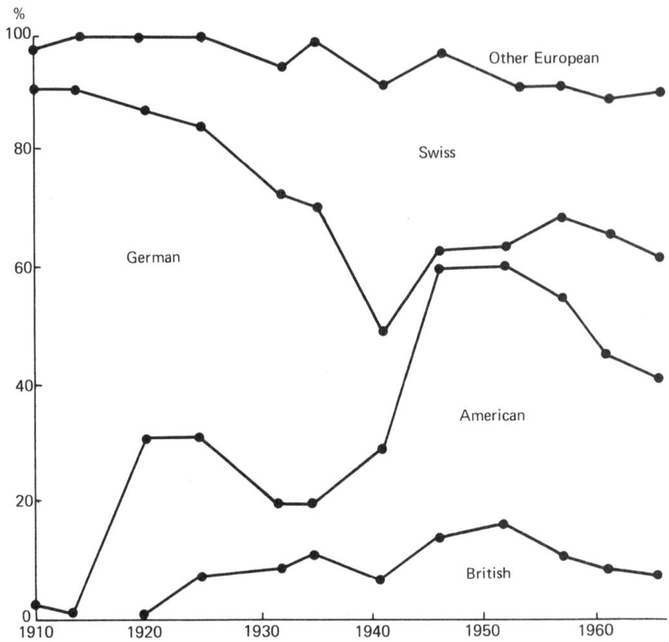

Fig. 2.2 Percentage of Patents by Nationality in five-year periods, 1910–1966.

Source: Reekie, op. cit., p. 256.

order to ensure adequate supplies of all the medicines available on the world market. They can buy the output of British-owned firms which is the result of British research. This, however, will give prompt post-discovery access to only a small proportion of discoveries. They can also purchase British production of non-patented discoveries. This is unlikely to raise by much the proportion of recent discoveries available since many of these are or have been patented (although this could be done on expiry of a patent). Access to the bulk of post-1941 discoveries promptly, which means well before patent expiry, can only be obtained, therefore, by the payment of royalities by British firms to overseas patent holders, or by direct importation, or by the establishment of foreign-owned manufacturing and/or distributing subsidiaries in this country.

The fact that 60 per cent of industry output is in the hands of foreign-controlled subsidiaries can thus be looked upon as one means of gaining access to the patented research results of overseas companies. From a purely balance of payments viewpoint, it can be said that as long as the relevant profits remitted by subsidiaries to foreign parents are less than would be the importation costs or the royalty charges which otherwise would be incurred then foreign subsidiaries do not have detrimental effects on the economy. From a total economy standpoint, the effect on the balance of payments must be taken into account, but so also must the loss in production of other goods due to the diversion of resources, including skilled scientific manpower, from whatever these resources might best have been doing had they not been employed in foreign-owned pharmaceutical subsidiaries. If from a total economy viewpoint these resources could have served the economy better elsewhere, then it may be that imports, or royalty payments plus domestic manufacture, would be economically preferable to foreign-owned subsidiaries manufacturing in the UK.

Whatever the truth, the presence of foreign subsidiaries is not automatically and necessarily disadvantageous to the economy.

It is also apposite to point out that several of the larger British companies have themselves established subsidiaries overseas. Burroughs Wellcome conducts research in Kenya and the United States and manufactures in all five continents. Glaxo also has overseas factories. Its Australian plant supplies New Zealand and the entire Australian demand for penicillin and streptomycin. Beecham, Boots and ICI, among others, all have overseas subsidiaries, and are continually increasing their overseas capacity. The traffic is not all one way.

4 Exports and imports

Exports of pharmaceutical products almost equal to the industry's sales to the NHS. In 1972 export sales, at over £173 million, were three and a half times their 1963 level. Imports were valued at £49 million, giving a trade surplus well over £100 million. Table 2.6 shows how exports have continuously exceeded imports over the years and Table 2.7, which refers to 1971, shows that the United Kingdom ranks second in terms of pharmaceutical exports. Moreover, the British ratio of exports to imports was higher than that of any other country.

It is, of course, no accident that the five leading exporters are also the five leading innovators of Table 2.5.

Moreover, the recent NEDO study discovered[1] that about 50 per cent of the industry's exports are contributed by the UK subsidiaries of

Table 2.6 UK pharmaceutical exports and imports (£m)

Year	*Imports*	*Exports*	*Year*	*Imports*	*Exports*
1938	1.7	3.3	1956	7.8	40.2
1939	1.8	3.3	1957	7.8	44.4
1940	1.7	4.9	1958	9.8	42.6
1941	1.3	4.8	1959	4.4	45.4
1942	1.1	3.8	1960	5.3	49.1
1943	0.8	4.1	1961	5.3	53.7
1944	2.5	4.8	1962	5.4	56.2
1945	3.2	6.4	1963	6.3	54.3
1946	1.0	12.8	1964	7.1	59.6
1947	1.9	14.6	1965	11.1	67.5
1948	1.3	15.7	1966	14.6	75.2
1949	1.5	18.4	1967	15.8	79.4
1950	2.8	24.9	1968	19.5	97.3
1951	6.0	36.7	1969	25.5	118.8
1952	4.5	33.7	1970	33.7	140.3
1953	5.7	32.5	1971	37.6	168.4
1954	9.6	36.0	1972	43.7	180.8
1955	7.7	40.4	1973	66.9	221.2

Source: Overseas Trade Statistics.

overseas firms which use Britain as a key export base. The same study estimated a negative balance on the 'invisible' account (i.e. international remittances between Britain and the rest of the world of dividends, interest, royalties, etc.) but nevertheless concluded that this did no more than reduce the overall balance of payments surplus to a figure of around £90 million in 1971.

This cheerful situation begs the question as to whether and how long it may be expected to prevail. If it is to prevail then three conditions, at

Table 2.7 World trade in pharmaceuticals, 1971 Leading exporters

	Exports *$m*	*Imports* *$m*	*Balance of trade* *$m*
West Germany	537.7	205.3	332.4
UK	410.4	91.6	318.8
USA	396.0	119.4	276.6
Switzerland	364.9	94.3	270.6
France	258.0	161.4	96.7

Source: ABPI.

least, must be fulfilled. First, British laboratories must continue to produce a satisfactory flow of the research-based discoveries on which exports depend. Second, non-tariff type barriers to international trade must not develop to such an extent that the pattern of supply to world markets changes radically. For example, already the effects of varying national drug registration requirements, different national tastes and fears of political action have given rise to the widespread carrying out of the later stages of production – formulation, presentation and packaging – within the individual market being supplied. Third, Britain must continue to remain a relatively attractive base for investment by the industry. To date Britain has had the advantages of a speedy system of drug registration, a satisfactory patent system, relative political stability, the English language, a highly regarded medical establishment and an availability of qualified scientific staff. The other side of this picture, however, as the NEDO study revealed, is that the prices received by the industry for its products are not only relatively low by international standards, but are drifting lower due to continuous governmental pressures. If this continues and has a corresponding effect on profits then 'both the incentive to invest in the UK and the supply of necessary funds would be reduced'. And it is on such investment and the flows of funds that R & D, innovation and so exports depend.

5 Industry entry

The attractiveness of Britain as an investment location in the past can be illustrated by studying the record of entry into the industry. Some of the foreign entrants, of course, may merely have established marketing and distribution subsidiaries in the UK. Nevertheless, some indication of the trend can be obtained.

In order to determine whether or not the community of firms comprising the industry was a static entity, an analysis of its age structure is given in Table 2.8 which indicates a continuous and fairly even flow of firms into the industry since 1950. Over 30 per cent of industry sales in 1966 were made by post-1949 entrants, large and small. Further, except for the five or six most recent entrants, there is no obvious relationship between age and company size. Unlike more traditional industries, both rapid relative and absolute growth can occur soon after entry.

Table 2.8 Size and age distribution of firms in the UK pharmaceutical industry at 31 Dec 1966

Year of entry	*No. of firms*	*Total GP sales, 1966 (£'000)*	*Average GP sales, 1966 (£'000)*	*% total GP*	*% age group sales by firm size grouping: Less than £1m*	*£1m–£5m*	*Over £5m*	*totals*
Pre 1950	45	80,576	1,701	69.2	15.5	55.1	29.4	100.0
1950	–	–	–	–	–	–	–	–
1951	2	3,548	1,774	3.0	10.3	89.7	–	100.0
1952	–	–	–	–	–	–	–	–
1953	4	10,488	2,622	9.0	–	43.9	56.1	100.0
1954	1	4,788	4,778	4.1	–	100.0	–	100.0
1955	1	1,222	1,222	1.1	–	100.0	–	100.0
1956	1	2,264	2,264	1.9	–	100.0	–	100.0
1957	–	–	–	–	–	–	–	–
1958	3	9.501	3,167	8.2	29.0	–	71.0	100.0
1959	2	408	204	0.4	100.0	–	–	100.0
1960	5	1,160	232	1.0	100.0	–	–	100.0
1961	–	–	–	–	–	–	–	–
1962	1	1,375	1,375	1.2	–	100.0	–	100.0
1963	1	60	60	0.1	100.0	–	–	100.0
1964	1	441	441	0.4	100.0	–	–	100.0
1965	2	329	165	0.3	100.0	–	–	100.0
1966	2	50	25	0.1	100.0	–	–	100.0
Totals	71	116,200	1,637	100.0	19.6	49.5	30.9	100.0

Source: W. D. Reekie, 'Barriers to Entry and Competition', in G. Teeling-Smith (ed.), *Economics and Innovation in the Pharmaceutical Industry* (OHE, 1970).

6 Diversification out of pharmaceuticals

Drug industry members participate in a wide variety of other industries. This section attempts, by reference to individual cases, to ascertain why firms diversify *out of* (as opposed to into) pharmaceuticals.* The motivation may be growth, increased profitability or risk-spreading. It is 'not necessary that existing markets become less profitable in themselves, only that they become relatively less profitable for any new investment the firm wants to undertake'.[2] Diversification is facilitated, or opportunities are provided, if certain conditions are fulfilled. For example, it is easier to diversify into a new area if production techniques are similar to those of the firm's primary interest. It is also easier to diversify if the new product line can be promoted by the firm's existing sales force since economy of selling effort will then be achieved. Third, the practice of R & D facilitates diversification in so far as it both acquires for the firm knowhow it does not at present possess with regard to a new area, together with the monopolistic, and hence attractive, potential of an innovation in an area successfully investigated by that R & D. Fourth, diversification is made considerably easier if a company can achieve this by acquisition of an existing operator in the appropriate field. The obstacles of lack of production expertise and marketing knowhow are overcome in one move.

Some of these points can be illustrated by reference to specific cases. For example, one formerly very specialised firm, the American Pfizer company, experienced remarkable commercial success in the 1950s due to its dominance of the antibiotics market with its brand of oxytetracycline, 'Terramycin'. Pfizer, however, has been singularly unfortunate in being unable to discover products of sufficient sales potential to fill the gap in revenue which is occurring now that its antibiotics drugs are (*a*) no longer patent protected and (*b*) have been partially replaced by the semisynthetic penicillins. When it has discovered 'winners', such as the anti-diabetic drug 'Diabinase', it has been beaten in the 'race to patent' by others who have made the same discovery almost simultaneously. Pfizer management has obviously perceived that profits would not be as attractive in drugs in the sixties and seventies as they were in the fifties. Since 1965 Pfizer's annual reports have emphasised that it is 'a diversified business', a phrase which is emotive of pride and possibly also of relief. Sales breakdowns by

*Intra-industry diversification amongst the therapeutic sub-markets is discussed in Chapter 3.

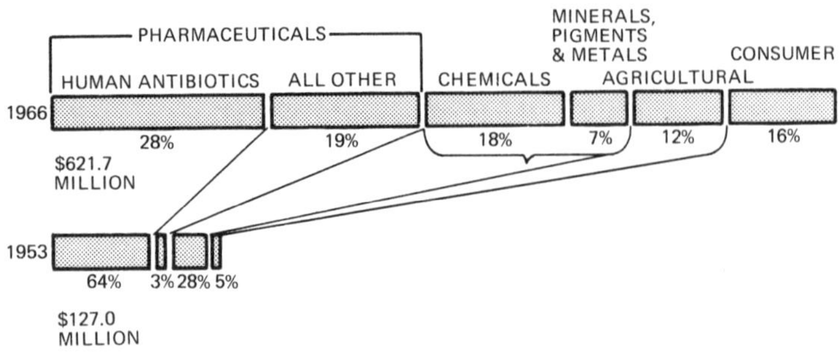

Fig. 2.3 Sales by product groups

Source: Annual Report, 1966 (Chas. Pfizer, Inc., New York).

product group are now prominently displayed as in Fig. 2.3 taken from the 1966 accounts.

As can be seen, Pfizer's dependence on antibiotics has shrunk from 64 per cent of total sales in 1953 to 28 per cent in 1966. This has been due to a diversification policy of both acquisition and research. 'Diversification through acquisition continued to bring new opportunities to Pfizer both here and abroad.'[3] 'Current research in widely divergent areas – medicine, organic and inorganic chemicals, minerals, metal, agriculture, toiletries, cosmetics, fragrances and consumer health – will certainly lead to significant product additions in diversified businesses.'[4] The initial diversifying steps in each case, however, were taken by acquiring companies in the field indicated in Fig. 2.3. In most cases, a somewhat similar technological base was present; some branches of chemical technology, and agricultural medicines in particular, share very similar research and production facilities to human medicines. Cosmetics, as well as sharing general chemical process techniques with Pfizer's other activities, also share a partially similar marketing base in so far as both are promoted to retail pharmacists.

Syntex, a Mexican firm, operating mainly from the USA, is also currently diversifying its activities. As with Pfizer a common technological base has facilitated the process, but unlike Pfizer it is doing so almost solely by research rather than by acquisition. The following statement indicates the development of Syntex R & D activity:

> In the early days the company's objective was to make particular substances whose molecular structure and biological uses were already known. ... In a second research phase, the company

> encouraged its creative group of chemists . . . to follow their own ideas. The result was a large number of new steroid compounds, which were . . . in selected cases, adopted as medicines. In the third phase which began in 1964 . . . the aim . . . is to learn more about how steroids . . . perform their functions in animals and humans, and to adjust the chemical research programme to serve the new knowledge.[5]

The second phase, now in its maturity, led Syntex into the ethical market away from the bulk chemical market. Now in the third phase it is diversifying into such fields as veterinary medicine, human and animal nutrition and fecundity and plant growth.

> Our growing commitment to active research programmes in animal health was symbolised . . . by the formation of the Syntex Institute of Veterinary Science. The goal . . . will be to augment the production of food from animal sources which is so necessary in the world today.[6]

> Future use of steroids may not be confined to the animal kingdom . . . evidence [exists] that the natural steroids existing in plants play an important part in their growth . . . the implications for agriculture are obvious, and Syntex has undertaken the investigation of synthetic steriods as agricultural chemicals.[7]

Syntex is thus diversifying in the directions its research effort leads and enables it to go. Its commercial success provides an almost unsurpassable example of synonymity of scientific and market potential.

The Eli Lilly Corporation of America is a company which, like Pfizer, relied heavily on the antibiotics market. In 1958, Lilly's world sales of ethical medicines declined from a high which was not reattained until 1962. Pharmaceutical sales have since risen continuously but not so quickly as other sections of the Lilly business. It would appear that after the sales decline a policy of expansion by diversification was adopted. In 1960, a complete section of the Annual Report was devoted to explaining why and where Lilly was diversifying.

> The basic idea underlying the diversification programme is maximum utilisation . . . of Lilly's resources. The criterion for entering new fields is: Does the Corporation possess talent, knowhow, production facilities, or other special resources which can be applied advantageously and . . . strengthen the company as a whole . . .

> In future years [Lilly] enterprise may be found in almost any line of endeavour which is not antagonistic to the corporation's goal of working for better health . . . for people everywhere.[8]

Again a common technological background was used to aim diversification into agricultural and veterinary products. Backward integration into packaging materials opened up an entire new market as well as providing a wholly owned source of such materials for Lilly's own use.

The industry is constantly evolving as firms are attracted into it, diversify away from it, or spread their interests into, to them, novel therapeutic sub-markets. Company diversification can assume either an inter- or an intra-industry pattern. At the inter-industry level, some firms, such as Syntex, are diversifying into these areas where their R & D effort leads them. Most, however, adopt the diversification policy they do because of a desire to maximise profits (either directly by being attracted into fields with an apparently higher rate of return than drugs; or indirectly induced through a desire to risk spread because non-productive R & D experience has lowered the perceived prospects of high profitability). Conversely it is unsafe to generalise. Firms such as Merck, Sharp and Dohme, with a long and still continuing history of R & D successes appear to be motivated by the self-same wish to maximise profits but their experience and expectations lead them to remain as relatively specialised concerns.

3 Patterns of Competition

1 Price competition

Economic theory can be used to predict the competitive behaviour of an industry. Where there are a large number of relatively small firms a high level of price competition may be expected. Conversely, where competitors are few (an oligopoly situation), a non-fluctuating price level can be anticipated.

The pharmaceutical industry has been seen to have a diffuse market structure but, contrary to theoretical expectations, price competition is rare. This is due to a number of factors. Firstly, firms adjust their strategy according to the actions of those rivals whose products are close substitutes. In the pharmaceutical industry this condition exists within the highly concentrated therapeutic sub-markets but is not applicable in the total industry picture. It can thus be expected from the theory of oligopoly that price inflexibility will be characteristic. Secondly, price rigidity can be expected from the nature of demand for the industry's products. Medicines are a necessity and as such an increase in price will drive relatively few people from the market nor will a fall attract very many in. The level of consumption is determined by the requirements imposed by disease incidence, not by price. As a necessity, medicines have an inelastic demand.

Under the NHS, this *necessity effect* is reinforced by the provision of medicines either free of charge or at a low-level prescription charge unrelated to cost. Thus consumers are little influenced by price. To them drugs are essentials, either available free or at a nominal rate. Thirdly, the necessity effect is complemented by the *isolation effect* unique to this market. Because of the highly technical nature of the products the actual selection of a medicine is not done by the consumer but by the doctor, a 'buyer' almost totally isolated from the source of payment for his selection. Unlike specialist buyers in other fields such as industry, he is not employed to primarily make a 'best-buy' in financial terms and he is not liable to justify his each and every action in terms of the corporate balance sheet. The doctor's isolation from financial responsibility extends until his overall prescribing costs are 'substantially above the average'.*

Finally, 72 per cent[1] of the market is accounted for by patented products. In this section price competition is effectively precluded since licences will usually only be granted at royalty rates ensuring almost equivalent pricing. Table 3.1 illustrates this by giving a non-random selection of the prices of some important drugs which have been subject to patent protection.

Due to the interaction of sub-market oligopolistic structure, the necessity effect, doctors' lack of price consciousness and patents, the poverty of price competition in the industry is not surprising. Having said this, it must be remembered that many drugs do fall in price. Some of these reductions will be results of some form of government pressure, while others will be attempts to 'buy' goodwill, either the government's or the prescriber's, for the firm in general. The remainder will certainly include some made by firms in the hope of increasing total revenue 'in the face of (empirical) facts consistently disproving their expectations'.[2]

There are, of course, the exceptions where the production of a drug identical with that of another producer will, at a lower price, encroach considerably on the sales volume of the higher-priced drugs. When this has occurred, however, at least three conditions have had to be fulfilled. The isolation effect must have been deliberately or accidentally minimised by widespread and prolonged publicity regarding the costliness to the NHS of the higher-priced drug. Secondly, the medical profession must have confidence in the quality of the cheaper drug before it will switch its prescribing habits *en masse*. Finally, this price competition must almost always be restricted to the non-patented section of the market.

The most prominent example where these three conditions held was in the introduction and success of ICI's 'Imperacin', a brand of oxytetracycline. Pfizer's patent cover on its own brand, 'Terramycin', expired in March 1966. ICI then promptly entered the market charging

*See pp. 104–5 below.

Table 3.1 Comparative prices of some equivalent drugs

Market	*Compound*	*Pack**	*Marketing company and price*			
Tranquillisers	Meprobamate	30 x 400 mg. tabs	Wyeth 4*s* 4½*d*	Wallace 4*s* 4½*d*		
Psychotropics	Amitryptiline	100 x 10 mg. tabs	Roche 10*s* 4*d*	Merck 10*s* 4*d*		
Diuretics	Hydrochlorthiazide	100 x 25 mg. tabs	Merck 23*s* 6*d*	Ciba 23*s* 6*d*		
	Bendrofluozide	100 x 2.5 mg. tabs	Boots 9*s* 3*d*	Glaxo 9*s* 3*d*	Leo 9*s* 3*d*	
Hormones	Cortisone acetate	100 x 25 mg. tabs	Glaxo 48*s*	Merck 48*s*	Boots 48*s*	Roussell 48*s*
Antibiotics	Phenoxymethyl penicillin potassium	100 x 125 mg. tabs	Abbott 14*s*	Glaxo 14*s*	Dista 14*s*	ICI 14*s*
	Tetracycline	100 x 250 mg. tabs	Lederle 65*s* 2*d*	Nicholas 65*s* 5*d*	Squibb 65*s* 3*d*	Pfizer 65*s* 2*d*
	Chloramphenicol	100 x 250 mg. tabs	A. & H. 74*s* 2*d*	Parke Davis 74*s* 2*d*		
	Erythromycin	100 x 100 mg. tabs	Lilly 38*s* 10*d*	Abbott 38*s* 10*d*		
	Lincomycin Hydrochloride	100 x 0.5 gm. caps	Boots 256*s*	Upjohn 256*s*		
Anti-TB agents	D. Cycloserine	40 x 250 mg. tabs	Lilly 54*s* 8*d*	Roche 54*s* 8*d*		
	Viomycin Sulphate	1 gm vial	Pfizer 13*s* 6*d*	Parke Davis 13*s* 6*d*		
Antidiabetics	Tolbutamide	100 x 0.5 gm. tabs	Hoescht 19*s*	Riker 19*s*		

Source: W. D. Reekie, *The Economics of Innovation with Special Reference to the Pharmaceutical Industry* (ABPI, 1971).

*Pack sizes have been adjusted on a *pro rata* basis to ensure that like price is compared with like.

37*s* per 100 x 250 mg tablets which heavily undercut the Pfizer price of 111*s* 9*d*.[3] By August 1968, the prices had fallen still further to 24*s* 10*d* and 38*s* 10*d* respectively, probably stimulated by yet another entrant, Berk Pharmaceuticals, in late 1966, whose brand 'Berkmycen' was selling at 20*s* per 100 x 250 mg tablets in 1968.[4] The isolation effect was minimised in this example by continuous Ministerial publicity about the high price of oxytetracycline and by ICI, which on introducing its cheaper brand stressed its own house name and nationality in order to convey to doctors a feeling of confidence in 'Imperacin's' quality and consistency.

Since the introduction of 'Imperacin', other firms, such as Berk, and more recently Glaxo, have introduced similar, non-patented antibiotics using aggressive pricing policies as a major means of establishing themselves in these areas. It would appear that the isolation effect can be minimised effectively and doctors persuaded to be price-conscious and prescribe accordingly. This conclusion, however, is primarily relevant to the non-patented market. In the patented market where products differ either marginally or substantially then price is only one of many product characteristics which doctors may or may not take into consideration. Even in the antibiotics market where much of this price competition has occurred it would appear that price-consciousness

Table 3.2 Proportion of GPs estimating the cost within the calculated price range for the amount of the preparation prescribed

	Calculated price range				
GPs estimate of cost	*Up to 5s*	*Over 5s to 10s*	*Over 10s to 15s*	*Over 15s to 20s*	*Over 20s*
	%	%	%	%	%
Up to 5*s*	62	7	2	1	1
Over 5*s* to 10*s*	24	52	18	9	2
Over 10*s* to 15*s*	4	22	32	26	15
Over 15*s* to 20*s*	2	14	23	25	33
Over 20*s*	–	2	23	27	45
No answer	8	3	2	12	5
Totals	100	100	100	100	100

Source: Sainsbury, op. cit., p. 191, Table 14.

has only become really prevalent since oxytetracycline's patent expired and other identical brands were introduced.

Table 3.2 provides part of the Sainsbury evidence on GPs' cost-consciousness in October 1966, several months after 'Imperacin' was introduced. This study took place several years after continuous criticism and publicity in the professional and national press about the costliness of antibiotics. Even then, substantial numbers of GPs could give no accurate assessment of the prescription costs of the one product they were 'most likely to prescribe' if presented with a case of the common disease, acute bronchitis, which is frequently treated with antibiotics (which in turn are also frequently prescribed for many other respiratory infections). The diagonal cells indicate the proportion of GPs who provided correct assessment of price. 68 per cent of the GPs questioned could not tell, within a 5*s* range, the cost of these prescriptions costing between 10*s* and 15*s*. 63 per cent gave incorrect answers on these costing between 15*s* and £1 and 51 per cent gave incorrect estimates on those costing over £1.

Promotional competition

Where price competition is unlikely or ineffective, business managers intent on maintaining or increasing existing market shares and/or profitability levels may turn instead to promotional and/or product competition. In practice these may overlap but for analytic purposes they will be treated here as conceptually distinct.

The industry's promotional effort is sometimes attacked for being unnecessarily high and for its allegedly poor quality. It is also subject to attack, because it is said to create or strengthen monopoly positions. The likelihood of this is particularly strong when, as usually happens, a product is promoted by brand name and through time the doctor comes to regard the brand name and the generic name as synonymous. This is relatively harmless while the product is still unique but on expiry of patent cover, or on the appearance of licensed competitors, the original medicine will be in a very strong market position if the doctor continues, albeit unconsciously, to automatically prescribe by the original brand name.*

Promotion is regarded by firms in the industry as an activity which must be conducted at some minimum absolute level, irrespective of size

*A fuller discussion on the implications of branding is presented in Chapter 5.

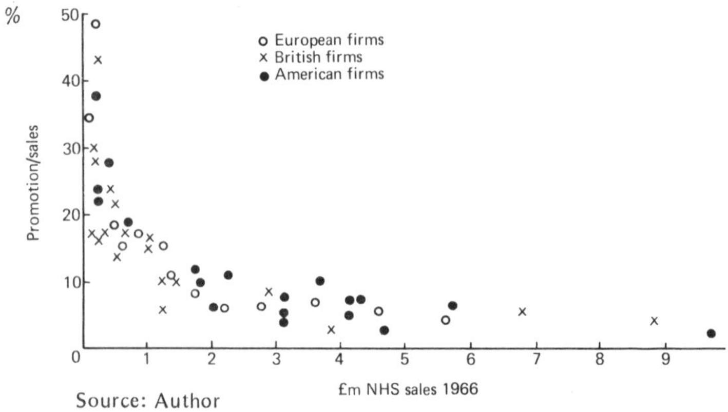

Source: Author

Fig. 3.1 Promotion: sales ratios compared with firm size

of company. The threshold level of advertising below which little or no results are obtained can be deduced from the 1966 activities of the firms to lie somewhere close to 10 per cent of the turnover of a firm selling £1 million. The minimum amount of advertising required must be sufficient to reach all 50,000 prescribing doctors or that section of them who prescribe for those disease classes for which a firm's product mix caters.

Fig. 3.1 illustrates clearly the effect of this threshold level on the behaviour of the smaller firm. In attempting to obtain viable levels of promotion the small firm of less than £1m turnover per annum is forced to expend sums ranging up to almost 50 per cent of its revenue income. This must certainly be a deterrent to entry into the industry for small firms and must make the continued operation of existing small firms a continuously difficult task.

No difference in promotional behaviour can be observed from this graph between firms of different nationalities of ownership. The pattern is similar for European, American and British companies. The continued existence of those firms with a high promotion: sales ratio would be in serious doubt were it not for the fact that many of them are subsidiaries of larger firms of British or overseas origin who are attempting to gain a foothold in the UK drug market. A small company with no external subsidisation and whose interest lay mainly in drugs, however, would be in a very difficult position if 50 pence from every sales pound had to be spent on promotion.

3 Competition by innovation

Pharmaceutical companies often have large research and development efforts. These produce streams of new products which enable firms to engage in innovatory competition – the 'competition which counts' as Schumpeter would put it. In the seven years 1960–6, 1189 new drugs were introduced to the market by the industry. Not only is the rate of introduction very high but the importance of these new drugs to the competitive position of the manufacturer is also great. Of the leading 150 drugs by sales value in 1972, 96 per cent were developed after 1947, and over half after 1963.[5]

Because of this high rate of new product introductions, the series of sub-markets presented in the static analysis of Table 2.3 is inadequate. It fails to illustrate the high degree of product competition which exists and which in turn ensures only a very short-lived period of control in any one sub-market. Thus, while demand for ethical pharmaceuticals is not very price-sensitive it is, on the other hand, highly sensitive to quality differences. This is especially so if the quality differentiation, real or assumed, is embodied in a new product resulting from a certain element of R & D effort.

Cooper provides evidence of the brevity of sub-market domination by any one product. He illustrates the necessity of product innovation if company domination of the sub-market is to continue. Such innovation must have clear advantages over the new products almost certain to appear from rivals' R & D laboratories. Tables 3.3 and 3.4 indicate that this does not always occur, and if it does it is frequently too belated to prevent a loss of market position. 37 per cent of the sub-markets studied by Cooper had product leadership (by sales value) changes in the period of three and a half years. In 32 per cent of the sub-markets leadership was lost by the original leading firms while in 11

Table 3.3 Therapeutic sub-market competition: changes in market leadership between January 1962 and June 1965

Sub-markets			*Number*	*%*
			90	100
Firms:	I	Change in leadership	29	32
	II	More than one change	10	11
Products:	I	Change in leadership	33	37
	II	More than one change	8	9

Source: Cooper, op. cit., p. 60.

Table 3.4 Number of firms dropping out of the first five ranked by sales in Therapeutic sub-markets, 1960–4

Number of firms dropping out	*Number of sub-markets*	*Total number of changes*
0	4	0
1	14	14
2	18	36
3	8	24
4	3	12
5	1	5
Totals	48	91

Source: Cooper, op. cit., p. 83.

per cent of the markets studied more than one change in class leadership occurred. Table 3.4 shows that out of a theoretical* maximum number of first five leadership drop-outs of 240, over 90 occurred in a four-year period. Thus while the sub-markets are oligopolistic in structure there is little chance, from a dynamic point of view, for long- or even medium-term oligopolistic domination to occur.

Since this is the case the great attention paid by the industry to R & D as a normal business strategy intended to raise or maintain market shares and/or profits becomes understandable. This form of competition may well be beneficial to the community. Assuming other things are equal, new and better medicines are evolved and, except in the very short run, the rigid pricing patterns of oligopoly are unlikely. In a traditional oligopolistic situation firms can be expected to assess the likelihood of new competition arising and will set a price just below the level at which such entry might be expected to be attractive. Where entry to an industry is easy (as its frequency apparently indicates it is in the drug industry's sub-markets) one would expect a nearly competitive price level to emerge. Cooper claims that if there are no artificial entry barriers then the drug industry may have 'as efficient a market structure as any'.[6] Price competition, however, has not emerged. Rigid pricing patterns have not been confined to the very short run. Suggested reasons for this and the impact of entry barriers on competition are discussed later in this chapter.

*In theory the total number of changes possible = 240 (48 x 5) but some sub-markets had less than five firms competing.

Table 3.5 Positions of 1972's leading ten products in 1965. Positions of 1965's leading ten companies in 1972 (all rankings by sales value)

Products		Companies	
1965	1972	1965	1972
4	1	1	1
3	2	2	17
13	3	3	30
31	4	4	3
*	5	5	6
22	6	6	2
*	7	7	10
5	8	8	15
10	9	9	21
*	10	10	49

*Out of the top 150 or not yet marketed.

Source: Intercontinental Medical Statistics.

Even at the level of the total market the vigour of this 'competition in creativity' can be seen. Table 3.5 shows that only four of the leading ten products in 1972 were placed in the top ten in 1965. A further three were either out of the top 150 or not available in 1965. Of the leading ten firms in 1965, only five remained in that group in 1972. The second placed company in 1965 had fallen to seventeenth position by 1972; the third placed to thirtieth; the tenth to forty-ninth and so on.

4 Diversification within pharmaceuticals

Members of the drug industry are liable to be overtaken technologically by their rivals or by new entrants. Sales depend on the possession of scientifically advanced products and these can rapidly become obsolete. In such an uncertain situation companies striving to maintain earnings can advertise, reduce prices, innovate or diversify. Advertising can increase a firm's sales but is unlikely to have much effect if the product is technologically inferior. Neither will price reductions be of any avail in similar circumstances. Expenditure on R & D in order to keep abreast of technological change is a surer method of maintaining earnings, if, and only if, that R & D is successful in producing products

Table 3.6 Diversification and market share stability

	Diversified firms	*Non-diversified firms*
Firms with a relatively stable market share	10	3
Firms with a relatively volatile market share	5	10

Source: W. D. Reekie, 'A Note on Diversification and Market Performance', *Journal of Economic Studies*, 1972.

in advance of rival laboratories. None of these three strategies, therefore, can guarantee maintainable levels of sales or profits.

Diversification (namely a firm's spread of operations within the industry between the various therapeutic sub-markets) does decrease the likelihood that the firm can be wholly technologically, and hence commercially, outflanked by rivals. No longer are the firm's eggs in only one basket. This assertion has been tested for a sample of 28 British pharmaceutical firms and the results are displayed in Table 3.6). The results support the hypothesis that the more diversified the firm the more stable is its market position.*

On the other hand, Penrose[7] remarked that changes arising from technological obsolescence 'are rarely so sudden and unheralded that the enterprising firm could not have prepared for them while its position was still strong enough to give it the advantages it needed to enter successfully some new field'. This would tend to suggest that in an industry such as pharmaceuticals, where large R & D is common, that the need for diversification as a bet-hedger is not great. However, it appears that R & D is just too uncertain an activity to guarantee commercial health. Specific examples of the dangers of being too highly specialised in a rapidly innovating industry and simultaneously failing to introduce adequate product successors are readily available. The American Pfizer company was a dominant member of the industry for much of the fifties and early sixties due to its drug 'Terramycin' in the antibiotics sub-market. Pfizer's share of the British market has fallen considerably in recent years due to its overdependence on the one therapeutic area and to the failure of its R & D effort to provide a comparable successor to 'Terramycin' in the face of innovatory

*Calculating the χ^2 (chi-square) to be 5.34, considerably higher than its minimum level at the 5 per cent level of significance.

competition from the Beecham semi-synthetic penicillin, 'Penbritin' and the later price competition from products such as 'Imperacin'. Pfizer is now diversifying away from antibiotics and could regain or at least stabilise its overall market position as a result of this policy. Products such as 'Diabinase' (licensed from the German Hoescht) have given Pfizer a leading place in diabetic therapy. More recently, in 1969, a major product, 'Sinequan', was introduced in the tranquilliser and anti-depressive sub-markets. The impact of this policy of diversification is quantified in the Chas. Pfizer Inc. final accounts for 1966. In 1953, 96 per cent of Pfizer's sales of ethical drugs were in the antibiotic field, by 1966 this dependence had been reduced to 68 per cent.*

5 Entry barriers

Earlier discussion in this chapter disclosed an apparent paradox. While entry to the various sub-markets was seen to be both frequent and successful, competitive behaviour as evidenced by price competition was still conspiciously absent. This author[8] has already suggested that it is possible to look upon the various sub-markets as merely a large number of simultaneous games of musical chairs being played by one unchanging group of large drug firms. When the music stops the participants in each game have changed, but merely in order to effect a mutual exchange of one oligopoly situation for another. If this interpretation of the evidence is correct, the the consumer of medicines in the long run is not, from a resources allocation viewpoint, faced with results similar to those of dynamic price competition but rather with a wasteful aggregation of oligopolistic short-runs.

Table 2.8 would seem to contradict the musical chairs hypothesis, however. There it was shown that there has in fact been a fairly continuous and even flow of new firms into the industry *as a whole* since 1950. There are two reasons why this has not ensured near to perfect competitive conditions in the industry. First the industry was growing rapidly in the period in question,† but more importantly, there is the evidence of Table 3.7.

Table 3.7 examines the origins of the entrant firms between 1950

*This reflects not only Pfizer's attempt to diversify its interest, but also the absolute, and so relative collapse of 'its antibiotics market.'

†New entry is not sufficient proof of the presence of competition where an industry is growing rapidly, although its absence would certainly indicate that competitive forces are weak. See, for example, Alex Hunter (ed.), *Monopoly and Competition* (Penguin, 1969) p. 81.

Table 3.7 Origins of entrant firms, 1950–66

		Market share (%) 1966	
	No. of firms	*Mean*	*Range*
Overseas drug houses	20	1.2	0.0–4.9
Related industries in Britain	5	1.3	0.0–5.7
New corporate entity	1	0.3	0.3

Source: W. D. Reekie, 'Barriers to Entry and Competition.

and 1966 and indicates that nearly all have been established firms (with the access to resources which that implies) and not individual entrepreneurs. This fact *per se* need not influence the impact these entrants have on the competitive behaviour of existing firms. But the fact that most industry entrants have been overseas drug houses certainly might. It may well be that a foreign entrant to the British market is seen as less of a threat to the existing cost/price structure of the market than is a potential British entrant. This could be so since a foreign entrant, by definition, is a well-established drug house whose competitive behaviour has already fallen within the behavioural group norms of the international industry. The world-wide concern at a political level over the price/output and promotional activities of the industry's members is too uniform and widespread to deny the existence of these norms. The desirability or magnitude of these norms is, of course, still open to debate.

The 'musical chairs' hypothesis could, therefore, still be relevant in Britain. In the last sixteen years the number of players has certainly increased but most entrants have merely come from another league where the rules of the game are exactly the same. Further cause for concern is provided by the evidence that only one entrant was a newly established firm. *Ceteris paribus* this would suggest that large resources are needed to enter the industry thus deterring entry, and by implication, permitting some degree of non-competitive behaviour.

What are the barriers to entry in the drug industry?* The principal *absolute cost advantage* of existing firms (i.e. when an entrant is faced with higher long-run average costs than is an existing firm) is the ability

*The classic work in this field is *Barriers to New Competition* by Joe Bain, (Harvard, 1956). We will follow his example and classify three main types of entry barriers: absolute cost advantages; economies of large scale; and product differentiation advantages.

of industry members to preclude competition with identical products unless royalties are paid to the patentee. In 1965 some 72 per cent by value of all prescription sales were of patented products. (Patents are discussed more extensively in Chapter 6 where it is suggested there may be a place for this form of entry barrier.) Nevertheless, other things being equal, there would seem to be little to prevent a firm entering the remaining 28 per cent non-patented section of the market.

Economies of scale appear to be largely unimportant as an inhibitor of entry. In production, unless the firm is integrated backwards to fine chemical manufacture or fermentation, then large and small firms can exist side by side at similar levels of efficiency. In promotion also there are no evident economies of large-scale advertising.

The most effective method of pharmaceutical promotion is the medical representative. At a local level there is no case to assert that the small firm's representative force need have less impact on a doctor's prescribing habits than a large firm with a detail force covering the country. Similarly direct mail advertising can be carried out on a restricted scale geographically. Journal advertising, however, may require to be carried out nationally since there are few regional medical journals. Even so, this form of promotion is not very important, accounting for only around 10 per cent of all pharmaceutical promotional expenditure, and furthermore the absolute cost is not prohibitive. (A full black and white page in the *Lancet* in 1974 cost only £158.)[9]

Product differentiation advantages of existing firms are the most obvious entry barriers in the industry and probably also the most effective. With over 2400 branded drugs available in the UK and an average duplication of only 1.1 brands per formulation the extent of product differentiation is vast. The entry deterrent provided by product differentiation is measured by the extent of the 'financial sacrifice' an entrant firm must incur to sway prescribers away from loyalty to existing brands towards the entrant's products. Existing firms will, of course, attempt to strengthen this loyalty and this they can do by emphasising product differences in advertising and/or by 'creating' new ones by conducting R & D to produce new, modified or improved therapies. Entrant firms can only revoke this loyalty, if to paraphrase Bain, they incur some 'financial sacrifice' not currently incurred by existing firms.

This implies, for example, selling products at an attractively cheaper price; promoting products more effectively; producing products which are different again from those already on the market, for example by initiating a successful R & D effort; or some combination of those or other 'sacrifices'. If existing firms are continuously attempting to strengthen the loyalty of prescribers to their own brands then a spiral commences. Entrants must cut prices still further; shout still louder through their promotional media; and make still bigger technical jumps through R & D, if their products are going to have the marginal attractiveness to shake existing loyalties.

Promotional competition, as a facet of product differentiation, is a prominent practice in the industry. It can be an insignificant obstacle to an entrant into the non-patented portion of the market. An entrant can gradually expand his promotional activities from a local to a national level as his resources grow apace. Physicians already know the attributes of the product in question and need be persuaded to switch brand alone.

In the remaining section of the market, 72 per cent by value, the need to spend highly on promotion is a very real barrier. The important question is whether or not the barrier is a 'natural' one, or is 'artificially' heightened by the activities of existing members. Products for this section of the market can only be obtained by paying royalties or conducting R & D.

In so far as national promotion is required to provide the market and so the funds for R & D (or a market for licence bargaining), high promotion is a real but unavoidable entry barrier and helps explain why all but one of the industry entrants since 1950 have been established firms. The suspicion remains, however, that this entry barrier has been artificially raised still further. Some firms maintain that 40 detailmen are the minimum they require to market effectively. The marketing manager of a large and successful British firm remarked to the author that it is an 'abuse of privilege' to visit a GP more than quarterly. This in turn necessitates a force of say over 75 detailmen, each man visiting probably five GPs per day. The implication was that firms can and do visit more frequently than the quarterly optimum and that the message passed on to the GP from the firm below the abuse threshold will be drowned in the competitive din.

Fig. 3.1 and its accompanying discussion also suggested that firms must promote at some absolute threshold level to make themselves heard. This has been shown to be partly due to the need to cover the national market to obtain revenue to support innovative activity.

However, it does seem probable that the minimum level of promotion needed to adequately reach all GPs has been exceeded by many firms and, at the same time, due to the interdependence of promotion as an activity, the minimum level has also been raised.

4 Research and Development

1 Medical and pharmaceutical R & D statistics

For the financial year 1972/3 total expenditure on medical research in the United Kingdom was estimated at £108 m. Over the years 1961/2–1971/2 expenditure increased at an average rate of a little over 13 per cent a year. This rate of increase accelerated to 19 per cent between 1971/2 and 1972/3.

Expenditure on medical research originates from three different sources: the government, the pharmaceutical industry and private benefactions such as trusts, charities and foundations. Estimates of the contribution made by each over the last decade are shown in Table 4.1.

In 1972/3, government-financed medical research amounted to £66 m. or 61 per cent of the total. This expenditure is financed through two main sources, the Medical Research Council and the University Grants Committee.

The pharmaceutical industry, during 72/73, spent an estimated £28 m. on research and development in the medical field. This was 27 per cent above the 1971/2 level. Practically the whole of the amount spent within the industry was financed by pharmaceutical firms themselves. About £1 m. of the expenditure was used to support medical research in the universities and other outside bodies.

The remaining £14 m. or 13 per cent was raised by trusts, charities and foundations. The Wellcome Trust (whose income comes solely from the profits of the drug firm Burroughs-Wellcome) spent the largest amount – £2.5 m. – in 1972/3, the Cancer Research Campaign over £2 m. and the rapidly expanding Imperial Cancer Research fund over £1 m.

Table 4.1 Medical research by source of finance. 1961/2 to 1972/3 (£m.)

Source of finance	*61/2*	*62/3*	*63/4*	*64/5*	*65/6*	*66/7*	*67/8*	*68/9*	*69/70*	*70/1*	*71/2*	*72/3*
Government	15	15	19	23	27	31	34	37	44	50	55	66
Pharmaceutical industry	8	9	10	11	12	13	15	17	19	22	25	28
Charities and trusts	3	3	3	4	4	5	5	5	6	8	11	14
Totals	26	27	32	38	43	49	54	59	69	80	91	108

Source: OHE

The rate of growth of R & D expenditure from 1960 to 1973 was faster than that of industry sales[1] at 9.5 per cent for the same period. Recent public announcements by firms (e.g. ICI) of continued major planned R & D expenditure increases give no hint as yet of any substantive changes to this trend. About one third[2] of the industry's R & D expenditure is incurred by foreign-owned subsidiaries in the U.K.; while world-wide the industry spends some £500 m.[3] per annum on the activity.

2 Nature and performance of pharmaceutical R & D

One of the major obstacles facing researchers in the industry is the still very limited extent of knowledge which exists concerning the relationship between chemical structure and biological activity. If this knowledge could be increased chemicals could then be synthesised specifically for a particular disease and accurate prediction of the efficacy, toxicity and side-effects of the chemical on the patient would be possible. Because of this lack of a developed base of scientific knowledge of aetiology, pharmaceutical R & D can only rarely use the relatively cheap, deductive or 'rational' research approach. Instead, the relatively costly 'random' approach to research must normally be employed.

New chemicals and organisms must be found, for example, either by synthesis in the laboratory or by the examination of naturally occurring moulds and soils for organisms not previously known. These compounds are then put through what has become a highly sophisticated network of bio-assay screens. Several species of animal will be used in each screen. The screens will test for any pharmacological activity present in the compound. They will provide information on toxicity, on side-effects, on the effect of one dose of the compound, on the effect of repeated dosages of the compound, and also on optimum dosage size to maximise efficacy while keeping toxicity within acceptable levels. Bogue indicated in 1962 that approximately 400 man-hours go into synthesis and first biological testing of one compound.[4] (This figure will now be substantially higher.)

At this stage no tests have been carried out on men and the results obtained from the animals may well be completely different from those which will be obtained when this stage is reached. 'In our present state of knowledge, prudence requires that man should be considered equivalent to the least favoured species.'[4] This almost certainly means that some potentially valuable drugs have been rejected prior to trial in man and also that some dangerous drugs slip through the screens and go on to clinical trials before rejection. Litchfield points out 'that a number of today's useful drugs (e.g. quinine, digitalis) would never reach a clinical trial in the present day atmosphere'.[5]

If a compound successfully passes through the bio-assay screens it is then submitted to a restricted trial in man, frequently members of the research team itself. Here possible species specificity with regard to man is thrown up. Toxic and pharmacological properties of the compound as indicated by the animal experiments are confirmed or denied and the performance of the drug *vis-à-vis* its clinical equivalents is demonstrated. After this initial clinical trial the knowledge of the drug to date is passed on to consultants in hospitals and other institutions for full-scale clinical trials.

Clinical trials require the skilful and informed use of the 'double-blind' technique: control groups of patients are placed on existing drugs or placebos while a further group is given the new drug. 'Double-blind' implies that neither the doctor nor the patient knows which group is a control at any one time. This minimises any subjective assessment of results or influencing of results by the clinician's or patient's attitudes. Unfortunately, since human beings vary from time to time and place to place, a laboratory situation with all variables totally isolated is impossible. This is one of the reasons why drugs acclaimed as a success after a clinical trial frequently fail to measure up to initial hopes when administered to a larger population over a longer period of time.

Occurring simultaneously with the later stages of the screening tests, the firm's R & D team must be working on the process of manufacture. Dosage form also must be determined and developed to act as a suitable carrier for the drug itself. It must be ensured that the carrier will take the drug to the site required. The particle size must be appropriate for correct dissolution time. The carrier must be made so that it releases the medicament either slowly or rapidly at the optimum rate. The correct dispersing agent must be chosen. With injection preparations, fluid consistency must be appropriate to avoid needle blockage.

Pharmaceutical R & D is thus a lengthy, complex and costly business. An increase in the supply and application of basic knowledge would of course cheapen and shorten the entire process. At present, according to ICI's research director Dr. I. G. Davey, only one compound in 10,000 which enters the screen ultimately emerges as a drug, the rest being discarded. An increase in the use of the rational approach would enable many such rejections to be made deductively without actual expensive 'suck it and see' experimentation; or even without incurring the effort of chemical synthesis. R & D effort could then be concentrated primarily on those compounds which were known to possess the qualities of a new medicine.

3 The direction of pharmaceutical R & D

Despite the fact that only 27 per cent of British medical research expenditure is incurred in the drug industry, it is that same 27 per cent which is responsible for most of the nation's pharmacological research. There are two main explanations for this. Firstly, industrial R & D, by its environment in a commercial enterprise, is geared to search for improved or novel medicines which are marketable commodities. Industrial R & D has as its principal goal, technological advance. Academic research conversely does not possess this environment. Traditionally academic pressures tend to direct such research to the increase of the existing stock of basic knowledge in biochemistry, disease processes, surgery, physiology and the many other medical disciplines. The fact that industrial R & D has still, in the majority of instances, to rely on empirical and trial-and-error techniques to discover potential new drugs, illustrates just how far research into the basic pattern of disease processes has to go before the product of such basic research can be of widespread practical use to the industry.

Secondly, as already suggested, the search for new medicines is frequently empirical in nature and so relatively costly requiring, *vis-à-vis* a systematic research effort, more frequent actual experimentation. The large-scale, rigidly ordered screening effort which this implies is best suited to the plentiful physical resources, both men and equipment, available to industrial laboratories. Conversely, this is least suited to the temperament of the many academic research workers who prefer to work alone or in small teams and with the minimum of direction.

The comparative records of discovery of industry and non-industry R & D support the assertion that most R & D directed at discovering substances which may prove to have novel therapeutic qualities is performed in industry. Sainsbury noted that 'the list of drugs in present use which have been discovered in university departments, although some are very important, is quite small'.[6]

Is pharmaceutical R & D misallocated?

A recent Labour Party discussion paper stated that 'we are very worried about the direction of [drug industry] research'.[7] This 'worry' is shared by others and centres on a concern that drug R & D is primarily directed at obtaining only minor technological advances. Such advances may be embodied in either the re-presentation of an existing drug; or in the combination of two or more existing products into one; or by a slight alteration of the chemical structure of a drug, 'molecular manipulation'; so that commercial advantages of uniqueness may be claimed without sacrificing any of the therapeutic qualities of the original medicine.

Table 4.2, analyses the new products made available in the USA in the period 1948–72. At first sight concern would appear to be justified. Out of 8219 new products only 767 were new single chemical entities. Of these 767 new entities some would be new salts, and some derivatives of known drugs, 'mere molecular manipulations'.

Nevertheless, the industry's R & D effort is not allocated in the way its output of new products would indicate. Sainsbury[8] discovered that two thirds of industry R & D was 'directed at finding entirely new products'. Only 9 per cent of the total R & D budget was directed at 'new formulations or combinations of existing drugs'. This is really readily understandable. New combinations and presentations are medicines on which the bulk of the necessary R & D expenditure will already have been incurred. The principal outlays necessary to synthesise the original drug, to test and screen it for efficacy and toxicity will all have been made prior to the original innovation. A relatively much smaller effort can be expected prior to the subsequent modification.

Combinations and re-presentations

Some proportion of R & D activity directed at producing combinations and new presentations is desirable. In an advanced society who is to say that the relatively small R & D effort involved in placing a highly unpalatable medicine in a confection base suitable for consumption by children is wasteful of resources?* Less emotively there is frequently obvious justification for attempting to present a drug, available in tablet form, in a form suitable for injection.

*'It is fundamentally in the sphere of detail of prescribing for the individual patient that the effectiveness of this branch of medicine [general practice] is accomplished, and in which the practitioner may gain personal satisfaction as well as fulfilling his long-established role; to cure sometimes, to relieve often, and to comfort always.' (Craig in 'Favourite Prescriptions in General Practice', *Practitioner*, 1967.)

Table 4.2 New products introduced in the USA, 1948–1972

Year	*Number of firms*	*Total new products*	*New single entities*	*Duplicate single products*	*Combination products*	*New dosage forms*	*New products plus new dosage forms*
1948	80	399	36	142	221	102	501
1949	84	389	40	147	202	170	559
1950	100	326	28	100	198	118	444
1951	86	321	35	74	212	120	441
1952	89	314	35	77	202	170	484
1953	107	353	48	79	226	97	450
1954	101	380	38	87	255	108	488
1955	124	403	31	90	282	96	499
1956	126	401	42	79	280	66	467
1957	127	400	51	88	261	96	496
1958	126	370	44	73	253	109	479
1959	107	315	63	49	203	104	419
1960	109	311	45	64	202	98	409
1961	111	265	41	33	191	106	371
1962	108	255	28	47	180	84	339
1963	89	213	18	43	152	52	265
1964	82	162	17	34	111	41	203
1965	65	119	23	23	73	22	141
1966	52	82	13	16	53	26	108
1967	49	83	25	26	32	14	97
1968	48	101	14	36	51	21	122
1969	48	71	11	26	34	12	83
1970	60	110	16	52	42	23	133
1971	46	94	14	50	30	30	124
1972	33	67	11	36	20	30	97
Totals		6304	767	1571	3966	1915	8219

Definitions:

New single entities – first marketing of a new single chemical entity, not previously known (includes new salts). Totals from 1961 also include new biologicals.

Duplicate single products – follow-up marketing of a new chemical entity, previously introduced by another manufacturer.

Combination products – any product having more than one active ingredient.

New dosage forms – if a product was originally marketed, say, as a tablet, ampoules, suppositories, etc., are counted as new dosage forms.

Source: Paul de Haen, Inc., New York.

The pharmacological advantage of combining drugs is evident when the result is one of potentiation, namely when the resultant therapeutic effect is greater than would be expected by mere algebraic addition. Even where this is not present there remain advantages. The GP can prescribe with confidence where a patient requires two drugs which are available in one combined presentation. Any incompatability between the drugs will already have been tested for by the manufacturer. For the patient there is a considerable element of convenience in taking one regular dose at regular intervals than, say, varying doses at irregular intervals.

Certainly no new combination or re-presentation will be developed unless there is a category of patients and of doctors who, for some therapeutic reason, prefer or are perceived to prefer the new product. Patient needs as measured by potential sales help guide the industry's R & D effort. This is the main cause of the 'worry' of the authors of the Green Paper. 'At present commercial criteria set the main direction.'[7]

One recent and very successful combination product was Lederle's 'Deteclo', a combination of three well-known and established antibiotics. Launched in 1969, it achieved a sales target of one million prescriptions in 1970. No doubt the authors of the Green Paper would argue that its success was due to 'expensive ballyhooing' and 'neglect of [other] possible lines of development'. Yet a glance at Fig. 4.1 is sufficient to show that 'Deteclo' was successful because it alone had the characteristics of a hitherto unoccupied market segment, viz. potency and cheapness. The benefits of a development of this sort to the NHS are obvious. The benefits to the company and ultimately to society are less clear-cut but more long-lasting. Lederle is one of the firms (like

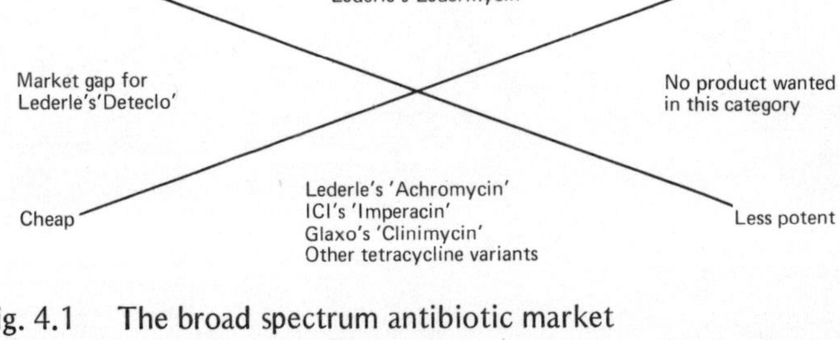

Fig. 4.1 The broad spectrum antibiotic market

Source: The Burroughs-Wellcome Marketing Research Department: cited by O. Palmer, *A Study of Marketing Management in Pharmaceutical Firms* (unpublished M.Sc. thesis, University of Lancaster, 1972).

Pfizer) which suffered most severely in the 1960s from 'competition in creativity'. Despite a large R & D effort it has, to date, failed to produce an innovation which will help it recapture the market leadership it had in the 1950s and early 1960s in the antibiotics market. R & D, however, is a long-term process. Teams of scientists cannot be expanded and contracted with the ebb and flow of a firm's market fortunes and still maintain peak efficiency. If minor products can be developed which both satisfy a genuine market need and provide a modest, if not dramatic, continuing flow of funds to attract investment and finance on-going R & D then 'commercial criteria' as guides to R & D effort are twice blest. They guide R & D to both major and minor societal needs and they reward the successful performer in proportion.

Molecular manipulations

It is because some discoveries have been suspected of possessing little or no difference in terms of pharmacological activity that charges of wastefulness of R & D effort have been made against industrial research of this nature. The products, while chemically distinct, thus facilitating claims of uniqueness for patent and marketing purposes, have molecular structures which are identical in all but one or a few chemical groupings or 'arms' attached to the main molecule. As thus stated, the truth of this charge is impossible to deny. The classic case is that of the similar antibiotics tetracycline, chlortetracycline and oxytetracycline. Laurence considers the three to be clinical 'alternatives'.[9] Fig. 4.2 indicates how closely related is the molecular structure of all three.

This form of pharmacological R & D activity is, however, no less prone to the elements of risk and uncertainty of outcome than any other kind of R & D effort. The resultant product of such R & D can be pharmacologically useless, it can be no more than a therapeutic alternative to the product it was intended to supersede, or it can be a major pharmacological step forward. Thus R & D of this nature, while susceptible to charges of wasted effort which can be substantiated by individual cases, is in fact no different from R & D of any other kind in any other discipline in that it possesses a record of absolute successes, failures, and 'non-successes'.

Molecular manipulation as a research technique must by definition suffer failures. As a technique which alters, only slightly, known existing molecules, with sometimes considerable scientific effort, it

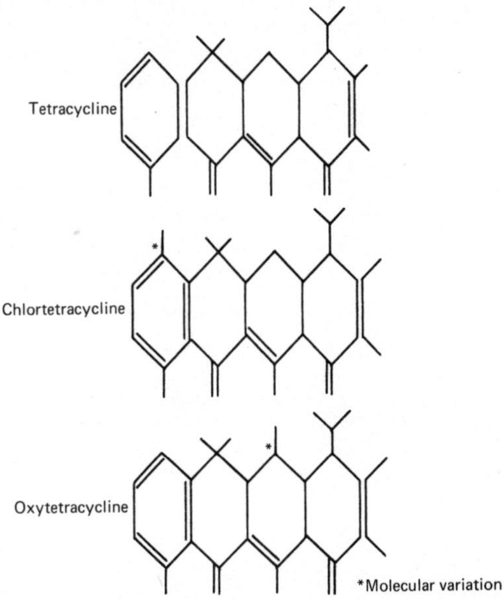

Fig. 4.2 Molecular structure of three pharmacologically equivalent antibiotics

Source: US Federal Trade Commission, Economic Report on Antibiotic Manufacture.

must appear to some observers to be wasteful of resources. Neither of these things in itself, however, is sufficient to condemn a technique as wasteful as R & D resources. Only lack of genuine success can do this.

One example of such success was the development of hydrocortisone from the original cortisone by the addition of what Calder calls 'nature's nearest approach to nothing', two hydrogen atoms.[10] The Nobel Prize winner in Physiology and Medicine, Phillip Hench, stated that this 'raises the effect of the electrolytes many, many times. And, if we were to ask the pharmaceutical chemist not to bother with minor modifications on the drawing board, we might miss some of the most amazing, hopeful cortisones that have ever been discovered.'[11]

The decision by Beechams to attempt to isolate the penicillin nucleus was taken with the deliberate intention of producing molecular variations by adding differing side-chains to the nucleus itself. One of the variants produced as a result of this effort is methicillin, a drug which can be used in infections caused by staphylococci resistant to both penicillins 'V' and 'G'. Another is ampicillin, a broad-spectrum drug, active against Gram-negative organisms previously unaffected by the older penicillins. It is not unlikely that further useful semi-synthetic penicillins will be produced by Beechams as a result of 'molecular manipulations'.

A long list of examples could be made out, but the very existence in it of a major success such as this, or even of minor modifications, such as the removal of some side-effects of toxicity from existing drugs, justifies the existence, at least, of the much disparaged technique of molecular manipulation.

Product and process R & D

Further criticism is directed at the industry's level of process research. It is frequently asserted that firms are more concerned with advances in the type of product available, thus allowing promotional claims of uniqueness to be made which will lead to a steady or increasing market share, than they are in performing process research with a view to lowering production costs with the concomitant increased possibilities of lower prices.

The empirical evidence certainly suggests that the bulk of pharmaceutical research is product- rather than process-orientated. Fig. 4.3 shows a slow but steady fall in the absolute number of process patents from 1949. (Prior to the 1949 Patents Act the patenting of pharmaceutical products was not permitted. New products could only be protected by the manufacturer developing and patenting all commercially sensible processes by which the product could be made.) Within four years of the change in the law, product patents had overtaken process patents and have continued to rise in numbers since.

Comanor suggests that this pattern is due to the imperfectly competitive structure of the industry.[12] In an imperfectly competitive industry, particularly one where demand is comparatively inelastic, as in the drug industry, the existence of monopoly profit margins will reduce the pressures to lower production costs. Lower costs, while enabling lower prices to be charged, need not lead to increased market share and higher profits for the price-cutter where demand is inelastic. On the other hand, the introduction of a successful new product innovation could raise or maintain a firm's market share. In a market with inelastic demand this is something a price cut on an existing product would not do, particularly in the face of a recently introduced

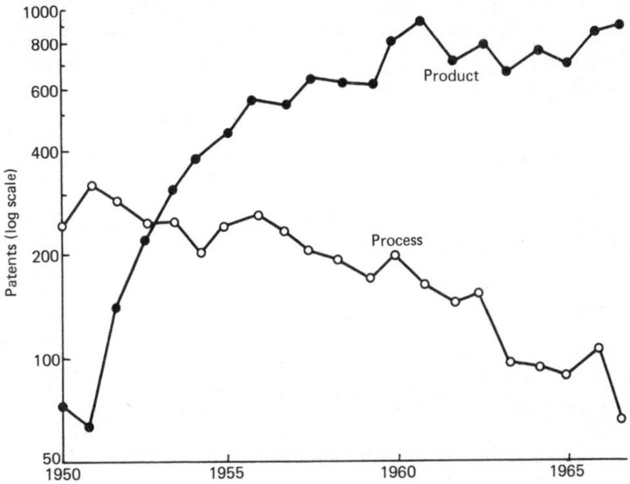

Fig. 4.3 Pharmaceutical product and process patents, 1950–66

Source: Reekie, *Research Policy*, op. cit., p. 257.

superior product substitute. The prevention of loss of market share is a greater stimulus to product-orientated R & D than is the prospect of profit gain through lower costs a stimulus to process-orientated R & D.

This argument is an explanation, not a justification. Cooper's emphasis comes nearer the mark when he stresses that the industry's 'products become obsolete too quickly for any real improvements in manufacturing processes to take place'.[13]

It is also probable that process efficiency prior to getting a new product on to the market may already be near optimum. For example, if a synthetic chemical drug requires twenty stages of successive chemical reactions to build up the required medicine, then, to obtain a yield at the end of the day of only 20 per cent from the initial raw materials requires an average stage yield of over 92 per cent. That is a very demanding proposition. An average stage efficiency of as much as 80 per cent would, because of the principles of geometric progression, finally yield only 1.15 per cent from initial raw materials. Thus the necessity for the manufacturing process to be relatively efficient prior to innovation also tends to lessen the need for the performance of process research, *per se*.

Process R & D does occur when the need (process inefficiency) and the opportunity (length of product life) arise. Market imperfections coupled with demand inelasticity tend, however, to encourage product orientated R & D. In view of what has been said, should this predominance be reduced? A value judgement only can be given. In this industry, possibly more than any other, the public interest is best served by the continued rapid increase in numbers of more potent, more effective and less toxic drugs. The failure to discover a new type of automobile or textile fibre may be measured in terms of inconvenience or discomfort. The failure to discover a more efficient method of producing a medicine may be measured in terms of waste of resources over time. And this is a relatively unimportant and small cost since (*a*) product life-spans are brief and (*b*) variable costs, the costs which process research may be expected to lower, are very low. The failure to discover an improved or novel medicine, however, may result in the opportunity cost of ill-health, or even death.

4 Trends and patterns in pharmaceutical innovation

Table 4.2, which relates to the United States, gives comprehensive evidence on innovation trends. The rate of new product introductions declined in the 1960s, from a 'high' of 559 in 1949 to a 'low' of 83 in 1969 and 97 in 1972. New single entities, the most creative type of new product, fell from 63 introductions in 1959 to a 'low' of eleven in 1972.

The OECD explain this on two grounds.[14] First, the industry, having successfully introduced treatments for a wide range of diseases, now has to concentrate its research upon the very difficult problems presented by the remaining unconquered diseases. The pathology of tumours and viral diseases, for example, is not fully understood. More importantly, both tumour and viruses act within the cell, not outside as do bacteria, making the discovery of 'Magic Bullets' more difficult. And in other areas there are difficulties in developing satisfactory models for screening and testing. For example, pathologically in rheumatoid arthritis no animal analogy is available. Second, the world-wide increase in restrictive legislation surrounding the industry since about 1960 has steadily increased in complexity. This has raised the cost of development and resulted in firms being more cautious and selective in their choice of products to bring to market.

An international survey of European innovations

Table 4.3 shows that in 1969 1543 new products were launched in Europe but that these were not distributed evenly by country of launch. This was not so much due to individual firms introducing more products in some countries than in others as to a greater or lesser

Table 4.3 New Products introduced in Europe, 1969

	No. of new products	*No. of firms*	*Single entities*	*Combinations*
Spain	481	230	115	366
Germany	235	149	49	186
Italy	216	133	86	130
France	170	115	57	113
Austria	144	89	49	95
UK	137	86	58	79
Belgium	98	70	65	33
Holland	62	47	38	24
Totals	1543	919	517	1026

Source: Author.

prevalence of innovating companies. Most new products were introduced in Spain, followed by Germany and Italy. Breakdown by chemical composition indicated that countries with the highest levels of innovations were also the markets into which above average levels of new combinations *vis-à-vis* new single chemical entities were introduced. In other words, only a certain number of firms in each market introduced new entities. Other innovators apparently rested content with re-presentations of new combinations of existing chemicals. The size of this latter group of firms fluctuates widely from country to country, possibly depending on differing national attitudes to combination products and to differing industrial structures in each country (e.g. compare the German medical profession's favourable attitude to combinations with that of the UK's now defunct MacGregor Committee; or the UK's maximum of 250 competing firms with Italy's 1200).

The new products introduced into each of the eight national markets are analysed by therapeutic class in Table 4.4.

An obvious point of significance is again the differing national dispersals of new product introductions by therapeutic class. Antibiotics accounted for 24.3 per cent of introductions in Spain and 13.1 per cent in the United Kingdom.* In four of the remaining six nations, however, they made up less than 5 per cent of all launches. As would be expected, cough and cold product launches were relatively more important in the north European countries of France, Germany, Austria and the United Kingdom, than in the southern countries of

*The Spanish figure is at least partially due to the multinational antibiotics firms entering the Iberian market for the first time.

Table 4.4 Analysis of new product launches by leading therapeutic class, 1969

France		*Italy*		*Germany*		*UK*	
Class	*%*	*Class*	*%*	*Class*	*%*	*Class*	*%*
Cough & cold	10.6	Hormones	8.3	Cardio-vasculars	11.9	Antibiotics	13.1
Hormones	9.4	Antibiotics	7.9	Cough & cold	8.0	Cough & cold	10.9
Cardio-vascular	7.6	Tonics	7.4	Derma-tological	7.6	Hormones	10.2
Derma-tological	5.9	Cardio-vasculars	6.9	Anti-inflammatory non-hormonal	5.9	Gynae-cological preps.	7.3
Ophthal-mological	5.9	Anti-inflammatory non-hormonal	6.5	Analgesics	5.1	Psycho-tropics	7.3
Antibiotics	4.7	Lipotropics	6.0	Haemor-rhoidal preps.	5.1	Haematinics	5.8
Anti-inflammatory non-hormonal	3.5	Dietetics	6.0	Gynae-cological preps.	4.7	Vitamins & nutrients	5.8
Sedatives & hypnotics	3.5	Cough & cold	5.0	Enzymes & digestives	4.7	Cardio-vasculars	3.6
Anti-spasmodics	2.9	Psycho-tropics	4.6	Ophthal-mologicals	4.2	Derma-tological	3.6
Psycho-tropics	2.9	Derma-tological	4.6	Antibiotics	3.8		
Other	43.1	Other	36.8	Other	39.0	Other	32.4

Spain		*Belgium*		*Holland*		*Austria*	
Class	*%*	*Class*	*%*	*Class*	*%*	*Class*	*%*
Antibiotics	24.3	Cardio-vasculars	11.2	Analgesics	9.7	Cardio-vasculars	11.8
Tonics	7.5	Hormones	9.1	Hormones	9.7	Vaccines	9.7
Cough & cold	5.4	Antibiotics	8.1	Derma-tological	8.0	Derma-tological	9.0
Derma-tological	5.4	Psycho-tropics	7.1	Anti-histamines	6.4	Cough & cold	6.3
Vitamins	5.4	Derma-tological	5.1	Cardio-vasculars	6.4	Gynae-cological preps.	5.6
Anti-inflammatory non-hormonal	4.6	Analgesics	4.0	Diagnostics	6.4	Antibiotics	4.2
Psycho-tropics	4.2	Anti-inflammatory non-hormonal	4.0	Antibiotics	4.8	Vitamins	4.2
Cardio-vasculars	4.2	Anti-spasmodics	4.0	Broncho-dilators	4.8	Analgesics	3.5
Lipotropics	3.1	Cough & cold	4.0	Gynae-cological preps.	4.8	Psycho-tropics	3.5
Anti-diarrhoeals	2.9	Diagnostics	4.0	Anti-inflammatory non-hormonal	3.2	Hormones	3.5
Other	33.0	Other	39.4	Other	35.7	Other	38.7

Source: Author

Table 4.5 Breakdown of 1969 innovations by presentation

Product form	*France* %	*Italy* %	*Germany* %	*U.K.* %	*Spain* %	*Belgium* %	*Holland* %	*Austria* %
Capsules	13.6	18.3	10.7	13.7	20.2	14.4	14.1	12.3
Tablets	41.4	30.6	46.6	43.2	23.8	42.4	43.6	33.2
Syrups	0	4.9	3.0	2.7	3.3	0.9	9.9	4.1
Injections	7.9	17.5	7.0	3.4	18.8	22.5	14.1	19.9
Suppositories	3.7	7.8	4.4	1.4	7.6	4.5	0	4.7
Powders	3.1	0.7	0.7	3.4	5.3	1.8	2.8	1.8
Creams	14.1	9.0	10.3	8.2	5.2	7.2	5.6	7.6
Others (ampoules, sprays, solutions, drops etc.)	16.2	11.2	17.3	24.0	15.8	6.3	9.9	16.4

Source: Author.

Spain and Italy. One prominent grouping, hormones, accounted for nearly 10 per cent of all launches in five countries, yet failed to be mentioned as one of the leading ten classes in Germany and Spain, and only achieved the figure of 3.5 per cent in Austria. Italy and Spain, the two southern countries, are the only nations where tonics achieved an appreciable percentage of all launches: analgesics reached the top ten in only four countries, Germany, Belgium, Holland and Austria; and in Holland alone did they emerge as a major area, with a rating of 9.7 per cent.

A few groupings did have a more even international spread. Cardiovasculars had a fairly high level of new product introductions in each market. And dermatologicals have also been fairly important overall. Table 4.5 analyses the new products launched in each European market by dosage presentation.

The most popular new presentation in each country was tablets. The second most frequent form of launch was capsules. In three countries, however, injectible presentations were as frequently introduced as capsules (Holland 14.1 per cent of each), or were more frequently introduced (Belgium and Austria). In Holland no new suppository presentations were made, while Italy and Spain had almost twice as high a proportion of suppository introductions as the remaining five nations.

Table 4.6 categorises the new products launched in 1969 by country of launch and by therapeutic sub-groups. The new products were then grouped into frequency distributions by country and by therapeutic class revenue parameter.

While relatively more sub-groups had sales of less than $1.5 million in most markets, the converse applies to new product launches. With the exceptions of Holland and Austria, most new product launches have occurred in the relatively fewer, but higher value, sub-groups of over $5 million.

Thus the 'worry' of the British Labour Party that most R & D is directed by commercial criteria would seem to be justified. Most innovations takes place in the markets where the potential rewards in terms of sales are greatest. Yet is it necessarily a bad thing that most innovation is in such therapeutic areas? Most people who fall ill are victims of common diseases, not rare ailments. It seems then to make both moral and commercial sense that most new therapies should be made available for the most widespread diseases.

And yet, as Tables 4.4 and 4.5 showed, a company cannot merely

Table 4.6 New products introduced by revenue size of therapeutic market, 1969

Therapeutic class revenue parameter $ million	*France* No. of C	*France* No. of P	*Italy* No. of C	*Italy* No. of P	*Germany* No. of C	*Germany* No. of P	*UK* No. of C	*UK* No. of P
0.0–0.5	18	3	17	1	23	2	23	5
0.5–1.5	30	13	34	17	36	19	20	5
1.5–2.5	18	13	19	10	13	14	9	10
2.5–5.0	23	23	29	22	28	47	20	44
5.0–10.0	31	45	27	68	21	41	10	39
10.0+	26	75	22	98	25	112	11	34
Totals	146	172	148	216	146	235	93	137

Therapeutic class revenue parameter $ million	*Spain* No. of C	*Spain* No. of P	*Belgium* No. of C	*Belgium* No. of P	*Holland* No. of C	*Holland* No. of P	*Austria* No. of C	*Austria* No. of P
0.0–0.5	55	19	37	3	94	23	116	23
0.5–1.5	43	62	38	21	30	18	28	45
1.5–2.5	19	44	21	8	7	8	4	16
2.5–5.0	27	146	29	21	6	12	–	–
5.0–10.0	7	54	19	24	2	1	–	–
10.0+	6	156	9	21	–	–	–	–
Totals	157	481	153	98	139	62	148	84

*C = Classes, P = Products.

Source: Author.

aim blindly at the largest therapeutic markets in a continent. This would spell both commercial and medical nonsense. It must be sensitive to variations in disease incidence, medical opinion and public habits country by country. These parameters will be reflected in the commercial demand for drugs in each country and may for example result in an R & D effort aimed at satisfying the Italian market by producing a new tonic in a suppository presentation. Examination of the Belgian market might reveal, however, a greater commercial opportunity and, *pari passu*, a greater medical need for a new cardiovascular drug in an injectible presentation.

Moreover, as the OECD pointed out, firms look not only at actual sales when allocating R & D effort, but also at unfulfilled medical need

Table 4.7 Take-off rates of new products, 1967–9 (success or failure 12 months after launch)*

Market	*Failures*	*Moderate successes*	*Successes*
		As % total innovations	
France	41.6	26.3	32.1
Germany	71.4	13.5	15.1
Italy	67.5	18.4	14.1
Belgium	95.6	2.7	1.7
Holland	96.6	1.1	2.3
Austria	97.2	2.8	0.0
UK	92.4	5.2	2.4
Spain	82.7	12.0	5.3

*The 4384 new products launched in the eight markets from 1967 to 1969 were categorised into three groups:
(*a*) Failures – those with sales under $70,000 after 12 months.
(*b*) Moderate successes – those with sales from $70,000 to $200,000 after 12 months.
(*c*) Successes – those with sales over $200,000 after 12 months.

Source: Author.

which in turn indicates potential sales. 'There are two groups of ethical pharmaceuticals which are not yet important in terms of sales, but which are important in terms of research efforts: anticancer agents – antivirals.'[15]

Yet no matter how careful a firm may be in assessing medical and commercial demand, innovation is still a remarkably risky process. Out of 4384 new products introduced into the European market between 1967 and 1969, only 282, 6.4 per cent could be regarded as 'successes'.

Table 4.7 analyses these product introductions by country of launch. The French market had an exceptionally high 'take-off' rate.* Nearly one third of all innovations were 'successes' and over one in four was 'moderately successful'. Germany, Italy and Spain were less exceptional markets but proved to be fairly favourable to innovators. In Italy, one product in three was a 'success' or 'moderate success', in Germany more than one in four, and in Spain a little under one in five.

Over 90 per cent of all products introduced into the remaining four

*The term 'take-off' is used to describe the speed of the product's sales level progression in its first year of life. The parameters used are purely arbitrary, but allow comparative measurements to be made. The reader should also be aware that comparative market sizes will also affect these results.

Table 4.8 Success rate of new products, 1967–9, total market related to chemical composition and nationality of manufacturer

	Failures (%)	*Moderate successes(%)*	*Successes (%)*	*Total*
Combinations	78.3	12.9	8.8	100.0
Single entities	78.5	10.7	10.8	100.0
Indigenous innovator	79.9	11.2	8.9	100.0
Innovator foreign to market	72.0	16.2	11.8	100.0

Source: Author.

markets were 'failures', however. In Britain, 233 products 'failed', only six were 'successes'.

Table 4.8 indicates that whether or not an innovation was a combination or a new single entity seemed to make little difference to its prospects of success or failure in the years 1967 to 1969 inclusive.

78.3 per cent of all new combinations introduced were 'failures' as were 78.5 per cent of all single entities. On the other hand, new single entities stood a slightly greater chance of being 'successes' rather than merely 'moderate successes'.

The new products were also analysed by take-off rate and grouped by origin of manufacturer. Indigenous products were regarded as innovations produced by a firm whose main operating base was in one of the eight countries studied (Table 4.8).

In the European market as a whole, indigenous products had a higher failure rate than non-indigenous, 80 per cent in relation to 72 per cent. Similarly, smaller proportions of indigenous products were either 'successes' or 'moderate successes' (nine per cent to twelve per cent were 'successes' and eleven per cent relative to sixteen per cent were 'moderate successes').

These figures could indicate that non-domestic companies tend to introduce products in foreign markets which are either already proven in their respective home markets or in which management has a comparatively high level of confidence. In other words, relatively fewer non-proven products may tend to be launched in foreign markets because of the higher costs of failure which will be incurred if the start-up and learning costs of operating in a strange market fail to be recouped.

5 Marketing

1 The nature of promotion in pharmaceuticals

The industry spent a sum of £28 million on marketing its products in 1965. Of this amount, £15.4 million was used to promote NHS sales alone. This is a figure equivalent to 13.9 per cent of the value of domestic sales and in absolute terms somewhere in the region of £300 per year for each of the 50,000-odd prescribing doctors.

The industry channels its promotional effort in a variety of ways. The major part, over 45 per cent, is undertaken by the representative system. Medical representatives are intended by companies to be their principal means of conveying information to the doctor of new and existing drugs. A representative can provide specific information for an individual doctor's needs more easily than can a printed advertisement. Representatives can also benefit both the firm and the doctor by acting as a channel of information or query from the doctor back to the firm.

In addition, the industry spends over 27 per cent of its promotional budget on printed advertisements, either in professional journals, or in mail shots.* Much of this is intended simply to be 'reminder' advertising – in other words, advertising where the persuasive element is predominant and the reader is intended to recall information provided on a previous occasion, say by a representative.

Over £1 million is spent on providing doctors with samples and a similar amount on 'other promotional activities', for example, educational conferences or the publishing of reference works of medical information. Table 5.1 provides an analysis of industry promotion expenditure.

*Most of this type of advertising is now (1975) carried out in controlled circulation journals distributed free of charge to prescribers.

Table 5.1 Analysis of promotional expenditure on domestic sales and total marketing expenditure

	1963		*1964*		*1965*	
	£m	*%*	*£m*	*%*	*£m*	*%*
Representatives	5.7	45.6	6.2	45.9	7.0	45.5
Literature	2.1	16.8	2.3	17.0	2.6	16.9
Journal advertising	1.5	12.0	1.5	11.1	1.6	10.4
Administration of sales promotion	1.4	11.2	1.5	11.1	1.8	11.7
Samples	1.0	8.0	1.1	8.2	1.3	8.4
Other promotional activities	0.8	6.4	0.9	6.7	1.1	7.1
Totals	12.5	100.0	13.5	100.0	15.4	100.0
Percentage of UK sales		14.9		14.1		13.9
Promotional expenditure overseas plus distribution costs of home and export sales	10.0		11.1		12.6	
Total marketing expenditure	22.5		24.6		28.0	
Percentage of total sales		18.3		17.4		17.0

Source: Sainsbury, op. cit., pp. 64 and 119.

Promotion in the industry is subject to adverse criticism on two fronts. The absolute amount is alleged to be unnecessarily high – 94 per cent of doctors interviewed reported that they received too much promotional literature (Sainsbury, op. cit., p. 143). In tandem, charges of misleading information and the use of frivolous material are made.

Some level of advertising is of course essential. When a medicine is introduced to the market the sooner doctors can be informed of its advantages and persuaded to prescribe, the sooner will patients benefit. Fig. 5.1 shows that while relatively new medicines are by no means the only ones promoted, recent innovations are regarded as the products requiring the greatest intensity of promotion.

Once a product has gained acceptance, there is still a need for some advertising of the reminder type. Doctors, like any other human 'buyers', 'do not have perfect memories; nor are they a static body: there are continually new potential recruits to be drawn from the newly employed . . . familiar products are from time to time improved or adapted to different purposes, and the manufacturer must make known

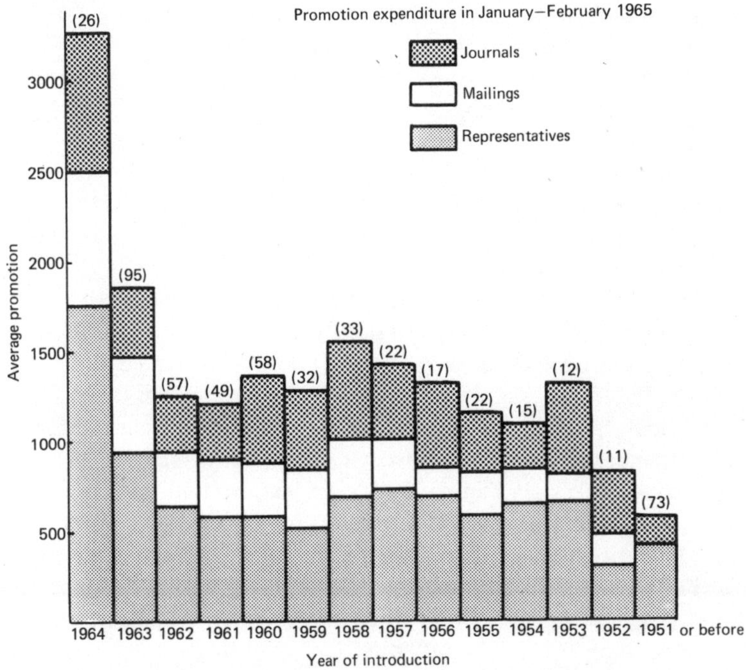

No. of products promoted shown in brackets.

Fig.5.1 Promotional expenditure per product promoted by age of product

Source: Teeling-Smith, *Economics and Innovation in the Pharmaceutical Industry*, op. cit., p. 65.

their new look'.[1] Fig. 5.1 indicates the comparative steadiness of reminder advertising on a product after it is accepted by the market. The average expenditure in the first two months of 1965 on products introduced between 1953 and 1962 varied only from £1500 to £1100 in the period of examination.

The establishment of a case for the existence of promotion is, however, much easier than selecting a level of promotional activity which is to be termed optimal. Inter-industry comparisons of the ratio of advertising expenditure to sales can be used. Data such as this, however, can provide only a basis for a value judgement on the presupposition that ratios for other industries are 'correct'.

Despite the waste of resources incurred when expenditure is unnecessarily high, in a highly innovative industry it may be better to bear some waste than suffer the costs of low diffusion of information and persuasion. In the Soviet Union promotion of new drugs is undertaken by the Health Ministry, not by the industry. Information about new drugs is usually restricted to mailed literature or journal articles. The information is frequently overlooked,[2] forgotten or ignored by the Soviet practitioner. It is neither prompt enough, voluminous enough, nor is there a sufficiently strong persuasive element, encouraging the doctor to use the new advances. The result is a substantial lag between the introduction of a new medicine and the obtaining of the incremental benefits by the patient.

One could deduce that despite the alleged antipathy to the quality of advertising literature received daily by mail that the doctor does in fact find this material of value.

The controlled circulation magazines which are distributed free to GPs and financed by advertising have full and non-antagonistic correspondence columns. Moreover, the ABPI provides a service whereby doctors can request that no further promotional literature be sent. Less than 4 per cent of all doctors have availed themselves of this opportunity. It may, of course, be that the service is little known and/or that doctors take the line of least resistance and do not trouble notifying the Association. Neither, however, would appear to be an insurmountable barrier if the profession were truly unhappy about the quantity, or for that matter the quality of the literature.

While much pharmaceutical advertising is accepted as responsible and informative, a considerable proportion is deemed by some to be the opposite. Representatives are sometimes accused of possessing little knowledge of a company's products. They may be briefed by learning verbatim a prepared script[3] and 'the essential purpose of the work . . . is to persuade the general practitioner to prescribe the company's drugs by serving him with *suitably tempting details*'.[4] Some advertisements are accused of utilising irrelevant techniques in parallel with exaggerated claims while understating or omitting comments on adverse reactions.[5] Misleading statements of 'before and after' therapy have been uncovered.* Samples too have been subject to abuse. Sainsbury cites their indiscriminate distribution by representatives to junior hospital staff.[6] Samples *per se* of course, have many commendable

*In one instance two X-ray photographs of two different, but very similar people, were shown in an advertisement of the 'before and after' type. No indication was given that the patients were different people and, in fact, investigation led to the discovery that neither patient had even taken the drug being advertised. (E. Kefauver, *In a Few Hands*, p. 74).

features. They can provide information of the drug in use, or can be used in an emergency or on night calls. Two out of three GPs in 1965 found samples useful or very useful.[7]

The need to both avoid dishonesty and maintain a high standard of factual promotion is recognised by the industry; and in 1958, after consultation with the British Medical Association, it produced a Code of Marketing Practice, a fourth edition of which was recently introduced. This requires that marketing activities must not be misleading and that sales promotion material must contain adequate and accurate information. Alleged breaches of the Code are referred to an ABPI Committee under the independent chairmanship of Sir Joseph Molony, QC. Should the Committee decide that a particular promotional practice be discontinued it requests the infringing firm to do so, possessing in reserve the power to refer the case to the ABPI proper who can withhold membership from the company concerned.

By August 1972, 108 cases had been laid before the committee, 57 originating in complaints from ABPI members, 11 from the Department of Health, and 40 from journals and other sources. In 18 cases judgment is pending or no charge was made. In 61 the complaint was upheld and in 29 was rejected. In no case has a company refused to comply with the Committee's ruling.[8] The number of complaints filed seems disproportionately small in face of the volume of criticism elsewhere – a fact possibly emanating again from the tendency of most doctors 'not to bother' and/or lack of publicity of the Committee's existence; and/or from the criticism itself being disproportionately large and being voiced only by a highly articulate minority.

The Sainsbury Report's Social Survey provided a more objective evaluation of the opinions GPs hold on drug industry advertising. 50 per cent of all GPs regarded promotional literature as an 'important source of information'.[9] Similarly 70 per cent of GPs viewed the representative as an important information source. Table 5.2 shows that 59 per cent of the doctors interviewed regarded industry promotion as the best source for providing them with knowledge of the *existence* of a new drug while 20 per cent saw it as the best source to find out about the *efficacy* of a new drug; and 45 per cent of GPs felt they could prescribe a new product after discussing it with the representative.

Industry promotion therefore, irrespective of its alleged quality, is doing its job of introducing doctors to a new product and providing information on which at least just under one half would prescribe. The fact that only twenty per cent of doctors regard it as the *best* source for

Table 5.2 The proportion of general practitioners selecting each source as the best one for finding out about new products

	Best source for finding out about existence of new products	*Best source for finding out about efficacy of new products*
Journal advertisements	7	1
Other promotional literature	10	2
Representatives	34	12
MIMS	7	3
Medindex	1	1
Drug firm meetings	–	1
All sources financed by the industry	59	20
Journal articles	19	31
Contacts with consultants/ other doctors	17	38
Clinical meetings	2	4
Refresher courses	3	7
Totals	100	100
Personal experience	–	16 GPs
Total sample	463	463

Source: Sainsbury, op. cit., p. 132.

finding out about efficacy is also as it should be. The industry concentrates its promotion during the introductory period, when comprehensive knowledge of efficacy is at its lowest. This intensity then falls off to reminder level. Reminders are intended to stimulate or maintain demand not only by 'reminding' the doctor of previous promotion, but, just as importantly, by helping him to recall previous experience with the drug in question. Since this is undoubtedly what will happen, whether the firm wishes it or not, then irrespective of cunning use of emotive techniques or unadulterated scientific information, the advertising will in the end only sell medicines which win approval on their own merits.*

*This assertion is given quantitative support by the 1972 NEDO study which discovered high correlation coefficients between an innovation's therapeutic significance, its chemical novelty and its resulting commercial success. (NEDO, op. cit., p. 105.)

2 Branding

Branding is an important practice in the industry; in 1965, 88.8 per cent by value of all NHS prescriptions were written out for products available only under a brand name.[10]

The Sainsbury Report suggested two major advantages to be expected if brand names were prohibited. First, more effective price competition would result; and, second, a source of confusion due to a multiplicity of names for the same drug would be removed. Confusion due to a proliferation of different brand names for the same product is more illusory than real, however. In 1965 within the total of 2403 brands listed in *Medinex* there were 2177 different chemical formulations: an average of only 1.1 brand names per formulation which can hardly be termed a confusing multiplicity of names for the same product.[11] The emergence, *ceteris paribus*, of a greater degree of price competition if branding were to disappear is, of course, indisputable. The crucial question is to assess the value of the benefits accruing to the community from this competition. The Public Accounts Committee attempted to measure these benefits in 1964/5. The Ministry of Health provided the PAC with evidence that if all drugs were prescribed generically then in only 25 cases would there be a possible saving in price due to a branded drug being dearer than its standard equivalent. In all other cases the branded drug was either the only version available, or it was itself cheaper than the non-branded duplicate. Of these 25 drugs, three had had prices agreed on under the Voluntary Price Regulation Scheme; and if a switch in prescribing had taken place from the remaining 22 to generic products only, this would have, in 1964, resulted in a total saving to the NHS of just over £83,000.[12]

Against the advantages to be gained from discouraging brand names must be placed the advantages provided by branding. Principally, these are primarily associated with identification of product. To avoid circular reasoning, these will only hold when duplication of product is present. (Duplication is present, in individual cases, to a greater degree than the average ratio of 1.1 brands per formulation would suggest.) If a particular brand is known to be satisfactory, the doctor can prescribe with confidence, and with the knowledge that his patient will receive a specific therapeutic agent. Generic prescribing may result in the same agent being dispensed, but there is no guarantee of this.

Differences in manufacturing technique and presentation form often induce differing physiological responses in the same patient from the same medicine. The *British Medical Journal* stated that 'there is a mistaken belief that the active constituent, to which the official name only refers, constitutes the sole basis for a drug's effectiveness. This is by no means always the case, the physiological response to a drug may also be a function of its pharmaceutical formulation.'[13]

This raises the issue of bioavailability, namely the rate at which a drug becomes available for absorption in the patient. This can vary with particle size, salt form, diluent, lubricant, compression of tablet and type of capsule. The more sophisticated the formulation, as in sustained release preparations or enteric coated forms, the more variables there are which affect the absorption rate. A further difficulty is the fact that conditions of absorption, metabolism and excretion may change with the disease process, and may not be the same in each patient for every day he takes the drug. Beckett points out that some of the most widely used antibiotics, steroids and anti-inflammatory agents (among many others) vary significantly, in therapeutic terms, one brand from the other, while still being regarded chemically and generically as 'equivalents'.[14]

The opponents of brand name prescribing suggest that the advantages could be retained and disadvantages removed if the brand names were abolished and the doctor prescribed generically adding, if he wished, the name of the desired manufacturer to the prescription form. Sainsbury in fact expressly states that it is 'important that the manufacturer . . . be easily identified and that the doctor should be able to ensure . . . [that he is] the maker of his choice'.[15] The sincerity of this last remark is questionable. Intuitively, it seems quite improbable that time-pressed doctors, who write out several dozen prescriptions per day, would even consider adding the desired manufacturer's name to the prescription. This appears even less likely when it is remembered that generic prescribing will in some cases entail still extra wording to specify presentation form.

If this is so, then the comment quoted above would appear to be merely a verbal sop to those lobbying for retention of brand names. On the other hand, if doctors would indeed prescribe on a large scale by manufacturer, it can be postulated that, far from promoting more effective price competition, rather more rigid and long-lasting monopoly situations would result. Currently, drug firms' promotional emphasis is predominantly on the brand advertised. Since the average life of a drug is short, the average length of brand-name-induced monopoly is also relatively short. When the drug disappears from the market, so too does any monopoly position it may have provided. If, however, brand names were to disappear and doctors were to be expected to prescribe by manufacturer, then a massive switch of promotional tactics might take place. The stress might well shift from product names to company names. In such a situation, any monopoly position or market preference created by unique name advertising would not wither away with the demise of a product superseded by a more advanced one but would last for as long as the firm cared to retain the position.

Moreover, under such circumstances, barriers to entry would be relatively higher. An innovating company previously unknown in the market would be at a marked disadvantage to a similarly placed firm which had built up a considerable goodwill to its house name. Doctors are used to having to assess the value of new drugs introduced under unique brand names. They are not, except in a few cases, very familiar with company names. Currently an entrant firm merely has to promote the brand name of its entrant product: a task almost equal in magnitude to that of most drug firms introducing a new product. If company names become as familiar to doctors as brand names are now, a potential entrant would have the additional barrier to overcome of inducing doctors to shift from existing, known company names.

3 The evidence of econometrics

This section reports on a cross-sectional multiple regression analysis carried out on pharmaceutical advertising at the level of the therapeutic sub-market.[16] It is postulated that the advertising level in each therapeutic area will be associated with the following variables: the degree of market concentration; the level of sales; the level of innovation; and the ability to distort information which is present in each of the respective markets.

It has already been shown in Fig. 3.1 that levels of promotion in the drug industry may well be an effective entry barrier. Here an attempt is made to ascertion if promotion is associated with that other common measure of monopoly, market concentration ratios. An *ex ante* estimate of sales was included in the model, first because promotion is obviously associated with sales, and second because management in the drug industry has been found to begin with estimates of sales and then to proceed to determine what promotion figure is appropriate for that sales target.[17]

The third determinant of promotion was innovation. Fig. 5.1 has already illustrated the need for a high initial level of advertising to obtain doctor acceptance of a new product. It might consequently be expected that those therapeutic markets with greater numbers of new products would also be subject to greater promotional activity. Fig. 5.2 illustrates a simple exercise carried out to test this relationship.

As can be seen from an inspection of the diagram, one therapeutic grouping, antibiotics, was *ceteris paribus* spending a disproportionate sum on promotion relative to the remainder of the industry. Removing antibiotics from the study ($n = 37$ becomes $n = 36$) the coefficient of determination, r^2, rises from 0.72 to 0.83 ($r = 0.91$). Thus while it could be suggested that innovation is a principal determinant of promotion in most groupings, in the antibiotics market, which alone accounts for over 20 per cent of industry sales to the NHS, other

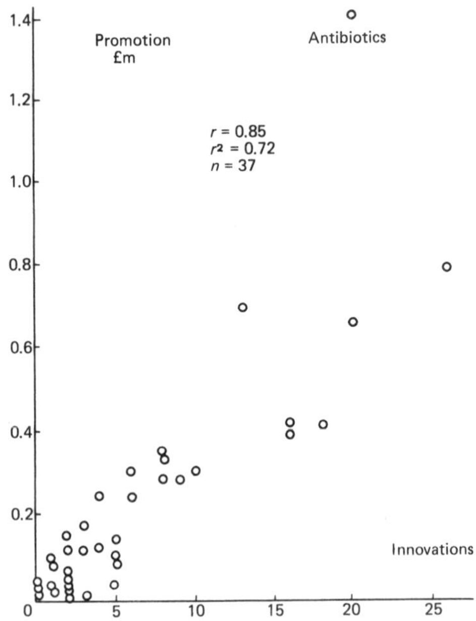

Fig. 5.2 Therapeutic classes, promotion 1966, innovations 1962–65

Source: Author.

factors are of much greater importance in determining promotional levels.

Finally there is the problem of distortion. Since advertising is alleged to have the ability to increase or maintain demand and since it contains persuasive elements it could be suggested that businessmen will be tempted to use misleading claims in order to strengthen this persuasive element and hence the efficacy of their advertising. If this is so, then *ceteris paribus* it would be expected that advertising would be heaviest in those areas where misleading claims are less readily detectable. This argument can be extended even to promotion by advertisers who would otherwise shun the making of any deliberately misleading claims or intentional dishonesty.

For example, there are still many disease areas where the therapies available are symptom-relieving not curative, and possibly sometimes fail to meet even this former claim. In such cases more promotion is possibly required to get doctors to prescribe than in markets where drugs have well-defined and easily recognisable medical effects. With fewer specific claims to promote firms are left only with the alternative of shouting louder.

The following general model was tested:

$$A_t = f(\bar{S}_t, I, M, D)$$

where A_t = promotion, $\bar{S}_t$ = *ex ante* sales, I = level of innovation, M = market concentration, and D = the state of technology as assessed by an independent panel of pharmacological and clinical experts.

No significant association between promotion and market structure was discovered. The remaining three independent variables, however, all had statistically significant relationships with promotion. The equation calculated was as follows:

$$A_t = 0.029\,\bar{S}_t + 18.938\,I + 56.666\,D + 4.146$$

The coefficient of determination was 0.878 ($r = 0.937$).

When the promotional figure for antibiotics was estimated from the equation it was discovered that actual expenditure exceeded its estimated value by 30 per cent. Coupled with the evidence of Fig. 5.2, this may indicate that antibiotics promotion is unusually and unnecessarily high. Moreover it is in this area that 20 per cent of all industry sales to the NHS in 1966 occurred. It is a preponderant market.

This may be evidence of wastefully high promotion. Certainly, there is no reason why each sub-market should have the same level of advertising intensity. (Antibiotics, in fact, has one of the lowest advertising:sales ratios.) However, the size of the communications job to be done, reaching 26,000 GPs is absolute and fixed. So although there is a minimum absolute threshold of promotion required to reach this market, once this threshold is reached there seems little reason why, other things being equal, promotion should reach the unexpectedly high level revealed in this study. Possibly the extremely large size of this market, and the associated rewards which go to firms which achieve a large share in it, has resulted in extremely high levels of inter-firm rivalry and so promotion.

3 Some recent trends

Brian Inglis, condemning the levels of promotion in the industry, asserted that 'demonstrably, they [American subsidiaries] have been the pace-setters'.[18] Inglis does not specify when the Americans were 'setting the pace', but it was certainly not during the 1960s. Table 5.3 compares the level of employment of medical representatives for three different sub-samples of firms surveyed by the author. The American sector with over 892 detail men in 1960 was by far the largest. However, at 69.5 per cent of all representatives this was not far from what one might anticipate given the American sub-sample's share of sales at 66.7 per cent. (By 1966 this situation had changed in magnitude, but only little in proportionate terms. American firms held

Table 5.3 Sales force size, 1960; NHS sales 1962 and growth rates to 1966 (1960 and 1962 = 100 respectively)

Nationality of firm	*Sales representatives* No.	*Sales representatives* %	*NHS sales* (£m)	*NHS sales* %	*Sales force growth*	*Sales growth*	*No. of firms*
UK	258	20.1	10.1	21.7	147	195	7
USA	892	69.5	30.7	66.7	116	146	14
Other	133	10.3	5.3	11.4	209	220	5
Totals	1284	100.0	46.0	100.0	129	164	26

Source: Author.

57.5 per cent of sample sales, and 57.7 per cent of sample sales force.)*

However, one fact in Table 5.3 stands out prominently and that is the very much slower rate of sales growth experienced by the American sub-sample. Three large American firms had sales levels which were almost static over this period, two of them actually declining. These firms specialised in the antibiotics market and were particularly hard hit by the advent of the British semi-synthetic pencillins. It was the behaviour of these three firms' sales levels which held back the relative sales growth of the American sector.

In 1962 one of these held 19.7 per cent of the American sub-sample's sales and 29.0 per cent of its sales force. A relative intensity ratio of 3:2 *vis-à-vis* the approximate 1:1 ratio shown by all three sectors in the table. By 1966 this firm's absolute sales levels had fallen by four per cent, and its detail force by 41 per cent, bringing the firm roughly into line with the 1:1 ratio, with 15.2 per cent of American representatives and 13 per cent of American sales in 1966.

It may be that the activities of this American firm, and one or two others like it, have given American firms, as a whole, a reputation for overspending on promotion. This information coupled with the econometric evidence might indicate that it is therapeutic area, not nationality, which leads to heavy advertising. The largest drug firm by sales in the 1966 NHS market was American; it did not operate in antibiotics, and yet had the large but not exceptional sales force of 86 men. Conversely, the largest British representative force in 1966 was 116 men; the largest American was 154 men, and both sales teams concentrated heavily on the promotion of antibiotics. It also appears from this evidence that successful competition by innovation, namely Beechams' semi-synthetic penicillins and Glaxo's cephalasporins may have helped curb this disproportionate promotional effort.

*This finding is in agreement with the evidence of Fig. 3.1, where nationality of ownership had no visible association with promotion intensity.

6 Patents

1 The rationale for patents

The two economic arguments for the patent system generally are those of disclosure of technical knowhow and the inducement of risk capital into invention and R & D.

The reasoning behind the *disclosure* argument is that an inventor, in order to obtain the monopolistic rewards accruing from an invention, will keep his knowledge secret. The granting of a patent monopoly fulfils the function of secrecy and prevents direct imitation which secrecy alone would not have done. Meanwhile invention and R & D will be stimulated elsewhere by the publication by the Patent Office of information on the invention.

Disclosure, of course, is not necessarily dependent on the patent system. But it does seem unlikely that altruism alone would prompt profit-motivated inventors into distributing, voluntarily, technological knowhow accumulated at some expense in their R & D departments.

On the other hand, it is interesting to note the differing absolute patent activities of varying industries. Where imitation of an invention can be easily and speedily performed, even when there is no disclosure, then the patent activity of the industry relative to all industry patent activity is high. For example, a new chemical product can be very speedily analysed by a clever research chemist and subsequently imitated in production. The chemical industry's patent activities, 20.6 per cent of all British patent acceptances in 1960, reflect this. Conversely, where an invention is difficult to emulate promptly or had a specifically tailored role to play, such as an aircraft component or part, then activity is low. Table 6.1 illustrates this, although of course many more factors, such as the inter-industry R & D pattern, contribute to the picture.

Table 6.1 Complete specifications accepted by Patent Office prior to sealing, by industry or industries, 1960

Industry	*All references %*
Engineering and electrical	42.6
Chemicals etc.	20.6
Vehicles (road, rail, air)	5.5
Shipbuilding	0.7
Metal goods	7.6
Textiles	4.5
Metal manufacture	4.3
Other	14.2
	100.0

Source: K. Boehm, *The British Patent System* (Cambridge, 1967) p. 176.

Patents provide an *inducement for risk capital.* It is a reasonable assumption that cash and effort will not be invested in inventive activity unless the prospective returns are commensurate with the technical risk and effort involved. If this is true for inventive activity, *per se*, it is even more true of development and subsequent market innovation. Generally this will absorb more capital than will the inventive act itself and to technical risk is now added the extra element of commercial unpredictability.

Patents are one way of providing protection to ensure that profits are not 'washed away' too promptly by a Schumpeterian 'gale of creative destruction'. Robinson, on the other hand, has claimed that the addition of patents to current market imperfections is an unnecessary extra. '. . . the year or so more's advantage of priority that early experimentation usually gives . . . [and] the subsequent goodwill that may arise from it', is sufficient to sustain adequate abnormal profits.[1] Market imperfections however, vary between industries and consequently the need for the additional protection which patents can provide will also differ.

It is also suggested that abandonment of patents might barely affect the current distribution of R & D, among large companies at least. In a situation of competitive oligopoly no one firm could allow its rivals to move technologically ahead of it. Thus, even without patents, the firm would conduct R & D to maintain market share. This argument is attractive but again inter-industry differences are ignored. If R & D is expensive and imitation simple, as in pharmaceuticals, then R & D might fall away dramatically leaving either a lethargic 'live-and-let-live' oligopoly, or a 'cat-and-mouse' situation where each firm carries out minimal R & D merely to keep a team together which can immediately set about imitating another's innovation should one appear. Conversely, if R & D is relatively cheap and/or imitation difficult, then sufficient monopoly profits may be made, unprotected by patents, to pay for and encourage past and future R & D and entrepreneurship.

2 Patent monopoly in the pharmaceutical industry

Four principal criticisms of the right to patent pharmaceuticals are made. These are:

(*a*) that it promotes monopolistic pricing and inhibits competition;
(*b*) that patents do not encourage pharmaceutical innovation;
(*c*) that pharmaceuticals are 'special' in that they are vital to life and hence price and quantity decisions should not be left to businessmen with a legally granted degree of power;
(*d*) that patents encourage only minor molecular manipulations to provide patentability but no therapeutic gains.

There are others, but most criticisms fall within one of the above groupings. Some are mutually exclusive; for example (*c*) and (*d*). However, they are not necessarily all put forward by the same critics.

(*a*) One frequently cited proof of monopolistic and collusive pricing of equivalent drugs when patents are present is the history of broad-spectrum antibiotic prices in the USA.* The price stability of these drugs, compared with that of earlier antibiotics where no patent cover was taken out and large numbers of producers entered the field, is compared in Table 6.2 which shows how rapidly penicillin and

*British examples include histories of drug prices when the patent cover has either expired or been compulsorily removed, when a greater or lesser degree of price competition has subsequently emerged. An example of the first is the case of oxytetracycline and 'Imperacin'. An example of the second is Pfizer's tetracycline patent, mentioned below. Similarly, the Ministry of Health examined the Smith, Kline & French patent on 'Furadantin', decided it was not valid, and instructed hospital authorities that they could legally purchase the product elsewhere. The price in 1962 was 374*s*. On this announcement there was an immediate reduction of over 86 per cent and by 1964 the S K & F price had fallen to 50*s*. (Cited in Inglis, op. cit., p. 161.)

Table 6.2 Penicillin, Streptomycin and broad-spectrum antibiotics prices, 1945–60 (USA)

				Broad-spectrum antibiotics (16 x 250mg. capsules)				
	Year	*Penicillin (10m, units bulk)* $	*Strepto-mycin (10g. bulk)* $	*Chlor-tetracycline* $	*Chlor-amphenicol* $	*Oxy-tetracycline* $	*Tetra-Cycline (5 brands)* $	*Demethylchlor tetra-cycline* $
May	1945	60.00						
May	1946	36.00	160.00					
January	1947	21.00	45.00					
July	1948	13.00	10.24					
Dec	1948	9.50	8.19	15.00				
Feb	1949	9.50	8.19	10.00				
March	1949	7.50	5.00	10.00	10.00			
Feb	1950	4.75	3.15	8.00	8.00			
April	1950	4.75	3.15	8.00	8.00	8.40		
May	1950	4.75	3.15	6.00	6.00	8.40		
Nov	1950	4.75	3.15	6.00	6.00	6.00		
Sep	1951	3.75	3.15	6.00	6.00	6.00		
Nov	1951	2.50	3.15	5.10	5.10	5.10		
	1952	1.15	3.24	5.10	5.10	5.10		
	1953	0.95	1.70	5.10	5.10	5.10	5.10	
	1954	0.75	1.70	5.10	5.10	5.10	5.10	
	1955	0.44	0.90	5.10	5.10	5.10	5.10	
	1956	0.52	0.75	5.10	5.10	5.10	5.10	
	1957	0.79	0.88	5.10	5.10	5.10	5.10	
	1958	0.70	0.88	5.10	5.10	5.10	5.10	
	1959	0.28	0.38	5.10	5.10	5.10	5.10	5.10
	1960	0.21	0.36	5.10	5.10	5.10	5.10	5.10

Source: US House of Representatives, Drug Industry Anit-Trust Act, hearings before the Anti-Trust Sub-Committee: Part 24, p. 13,664

streptomycin prices were driven down to little more than a marginal cost level.

To argue against patents for pharmaceuticals at this level, however, is inadequate. Oligopoly in therapeutic markets, strengthened by patents or the lack of price competition, is a fact. This, after all, is the function of a patent, to award monopoly in exchange for innovation. If abuse of monopoly is deemed to have occurred in any particular case, then the law provides for this.

(*b*) Inglis claims that the Kefauver Report 'exploded the myth'[2] that patents were essential for innovation. To support this view he cites the Report, which indicates, according to him, the 'overwhelming evidence that new drugs discovered in countries without product patents outnumbered those discovered in countries with such protection by about ten to one'.[3] On this point both the Report and Inglis' conclusion have been discredited. The Report completely misunderstood the nature of product-by-process patents available for drugs in Switzerland, Germany and elsewhere.

Cooper[4] highlighted the misleading implication of Inglis' statement. Of the 176 drugs studied, 79 were 'non-foreign' (being American) which, if included by Inglis, would have substantially altered his 'ten to one' ratio without any alteration being made to increase the accuracy of the Report itself. In fact if the Report data are amended to include product-by-process patents, then not one of the 176 drugs was discovered in a country without pharmaceutical patent protection.

(*c*) The third criticism listed, that pharmaceuticals are 'special' in that they are vital necessities, introduces social and emotional problems to the economic debate. Why such considerations should be introduced with regard to drugs and not other 'vital' innovations such as parachutes or machine safety guards is not logically apparent. The morality of the criticism is indisputable and it is, of course, wrong that some members of the community should be deprived of medical care due to price/output decisions of patent-protected businessmen. However, to cite Professor John Jewkes, 'the sensible approach to this kind of situation is, of course, not to abolish the incentives to innovation but to handle special cases of hardship by discriminating public aid'.

(*d*) The fourth criticism is possibly the most thorny of all. In so far as 'mere molecular manipulation' is beneficial, then so is the possibility of patenting which presumably encourages it. This will be so until the point where the marginal benefits of molecular manipulation equal the marginal social costs of patenting; including all the prior R & D activity and subsequent monopolistic costs which go with that patenting. Where that point is can only be indicated by either opinionative judgements at worst, or *a priori* reasoning at best. The suggestion could be made, however, in the light of the discussion on Sections 14 and 33 below, that this point may have been overtaken.

3 Provisions to counter abuse

British patent law is currently embodied in the 1949 Act. It awards monopoly rights and, in certain Sections explicitly acknowledges that abuses of monopoly are not in the public interest. The Sections in question, however, do not compel the patentee to cease and desist from his abuse of patent privilege. Rather they merely permit market forces to operate to help cure the abuse. If market forces fail to operate or do not operate in sufficient strength, there is nothing further the Comptroller of Patents can do about the situation. The problem would then presumably fall within the orbit of the Fair Trading Act.

The relevant Sections are 37, 41, 46, 14 and 33.

I *Section 37* provides that at any time three years after the date of sealing a patent the Comptroller may grant a Compulsory Licence to a potential user of the invention on request. That is, on proof of abuse by the patentee, the Comptroller will provide a licence, at an agreed royalty rate, for a third party to work the patent.

The grounds for issuing compulsory licences include:

(*a*) Non-working or insufficient working of the patent in the UK.
(*b*) If demand is not reasonably met at reasonable conditions.
(*c*) If commercial working of the patent is prevented or hindered by importation of the patented article.
(*d*) Refusal of reasonable licensing conditions or terms resulting in loss of exports, the hinderance of technical progress or the retardation of industrial development in the UK.

It is not the Comptroller's function to seek out these abuses, however, and the onus rests on the applicant for compulsory licence to bring them to his attention.

II *Section 41,* unlike Section 37, applies only to food and medicines and is much more rigorous in its impact on the patentee. Under Section 41, a compulsory licence can be applied for *immediately* after sealing and there is no need for the applicant to bring to the Comptroller's attention abuse of monopoly right. Under Section 41 the Comptroller is only called in to settle the terms of the licence, which he will not refuse unless there are 'good reasons'.

This singling out of food and medicines originated in and was inherited from the earlier 1919 Act. During the 1914–18 War it was feared that supplies in these vital industries were coming to be dominated, directly or with patent protection, by overseas control. Discrimination against medicines in this way is by now anomalous and the Banks Committee[5] has recommended its repeal.

III *Section 46* defines the extent of Crown User Rights. It allows any government department, or persons authorised by the same, to make, use and exercise any patented invention 'for the services of the Crown'. When Section 46 is invoked, the patentee is in a position to claim compensation for this breach of his monopoly status. Initially Crown user rights were thought to be applicable only in national emergencies or in matters concerned with the defence of the realm. Case experience has broadened this interpretation. Although the nationalised industries have generally been excluded from the 'services of the Crown', it is now clear that medicines provided to the hospital services of the NHS are included.

In 1961 the Minister of Health, Mr Enoch Powell, authorised the importation of tetracycline for use in the hospital services of the NHS. The manufacturers of the drug were not licensed to do so by Pfizer, the patentee. Pfizer challenged the legality of supplying the tetracycline, which the Minister justified by claiming that hospital services were Crown users. The House of Lords upheld the Minister's claim (by a 3:2 majority verdict), and the importation of the tetracycline, at a price considerably lower than Pfizer's, continued. The outcome of the case is interesting. Pfizer was paid compensatory royalties by the Ministry. Tetracycline's price fell dramatically after 1961, thus accomplishing one of the Minister's objectives when he invoked Section 46, the lowering of an unreasonably high monopoly price. (At the time of the controversy Pfizer's tender price was £60 per 1000 tablets, DDSA Pharmaceutical's price for the same quantity was £6 10*s*.)

However, this use of Section 46 and its success seems, *ex post facto*, to have rested more on its potential rather than its actual introduction of competition, since (*a*) hospitals only account for some 15 per cent of the nation's medicine market, the remaining 85 per cent being GP-prescribed, which was not then regarded as a Crown Service; and (*b*) some of the imported drugs were shortly found to be defective in efficacy and consistency and importation of unlicensed drugs fell away. In fact no unlicensed drugs have been imported under Section 46 since 1965.

Use of Section 46 in this manner can be argued to be unfair discrimination against one industry. If applied generally, it gives the government the hitherto unused and unexpected bargaining weapon of threatened patent curtailment and also potentially gives an unfair advantage to government purchasers over private buyers of patented articles from whatever industry.*

The Banks Committee, however, has recommended that Section 46 be retained as a 'sanction', specifically for use against the pharmaceutical industry, which can be used on a 'selective basis' if the Department of Health is of the opinion that a patentee's prices are too high.

It is difficult to understand why a Committee, examining the patent system in general, should spend so much time examining the effect of patents on one particular industry. It is even more difficult to appreciate the objectivity of such an examination when its recommendations are not based on a comprehensive study of the issues surrounding pricing decisions in the industry. The Banks Report makes no mention of the impact of the Fair Trading Act on drug prices. An even more glaring omission is its failure to discuss the VPRS,† and why it considers (implicitly at least) the VPRS to be an inadequate means of price control which must be strengthened by the threat of use of Section 46.

IV *Sections 14 and 33* perform a different function from 37 and 41. In the latter, the aim is to permit some degree of economic competitiveness. Sections 14 and 33, however, provide the opportunity to ensure that patents are technically 'competitive', or, in other words, are considered worthy by the patentee's rivals to be granted patent protection. Section 14 permits interested parties to oppose the grant of a patent after publication of the specification and prior to sealing. Section 33 permits third parties to begin proceedings against a sealed patent, with a view to revoking that patent, within twelve months after sealing. Effectively the two sections are similar except in the time

*The Health Services and Public Health Act of 1968 extended the scope of Section 46 to the production and supply of drugs and medicines required for use in the general medical and pharmaceutical services of the NHS. This was a direct result of a recommendation in the Sainsbury Report.

†See Chapter 7, p. 102.

periods in which opposition or revocation proceedings can be commenced. Revocations could be regarded as 'belated oppositions' and following the example of Boehm[6] they will both simply be termed here as 'oppositions'.

Grounds for opposition include:[7]

(*a*) If the patentee is not the true and first inventor or his assignee.
(*b*) Prior publication and other priority claims.
(*c*) Obviousness, lack of novelty, inutility.
(*d*) Insufficiently descriptive specification, or ambiguity of definition.

A discussion on Sections 14 and 33

The Economist pointed out that Sections 14 and 33 'provide the occasion for the only worthwhile examination [undertaken] of the merits of alleged inventions'.[8] Because of this, Boehm and Silberston express a wish that the Sections were used more frequently.[9] Only 2 per cent of all patent acceptances were opposed between 1951 and 1964.

This is surprisingly low particularly in view of the successful outcomes which opposition proceedings frequently have. Between 1950 and 1966 in pharmaceuticals, of 468 opposition proceedings, 359, over 75 per cent, had more or less successful results. This is shown in Table 6.3.

Boehm discovered that the chemical industry had one of the highest propensities to oppose of all industries. Table 6.4, relating to some major members of the pharmaceutical industry, indicates a similarly above-average opposition propensity in the pharmaceutical branch of the chemical industry.

As would be expected, there is a strong association between oppositions begun and oppositions defended, both of which in turn are correlated with patents taken out. Intuitively, it would seem apparent that a firm with a larger number of patents than another would also be opposed more frequently and conversely would be provided with the need to oppose others more frequently. This assertion appears to be supported by Table 6.4.

Absolute opposition rates, however, are very low in pharmaceuticals as elsewhere. Unfortunately the product content of the patents involved in the oppositions is unknown. But if the patents involved in oppositions relate only to run of the mill inventions then a propensity to oppose of around three per cent is an irrelevancy given that most patents are for such minor modifications. It is, *a priori*, unlikely that

Table 6.3 Pharmaceutical patents actions and outcomes* under Sections 14 and 33

	Section 14		*Section 33*	
Year	*Total Actions*	*Successful actions*	*Total Actions*	*Successful actions*
1950	6	6	2	1
1951	12	7	1	1
1952	18	14	0	0
1953	12	12	0	0
1954	14	13	5	3
1955	9	7	1	1
1956	16	11	0	0
1957	30	24	4	2
1958	33	28	5	3
1959	23	16	6	6
1960	47	36	3	3
1961	37	25	2	1
1962	24	17	2	2
1963	48	38	6	4
1964	24	19	7	3
1965	27	21	3	1
1966	37	32	4	2
Totals	417	326	51	33

*Actions refers to patents opposed, not the number of opposers; since several parties can and do oppose one patent. 'Successful' actions include those resulting in orders to amend the specification of the patent and/or voluntary withdrawals of the patent application.

Source: Author.

firms holding patents over a run of the mill invention will take the trouble of opposing another patentee. A minor technical step forward will almost certainly possess only slight competitive advantages over its predecessor, and the firm will expect, in the course of events, to be soon overtaken by another small step, which will also be only marginally more competitive. Patent cover in such situations will be of only minor value. Opposition, *a priori*, is more likely to occur when a patentee sees a real threat – as when the firm is in possession of patent cover over a major technical innovation providing him currently or potentially with a large element of commercial success. The converse of this, of course, is that patentees of large inventive steps are unlikely to be opposed (except where another laboratory has been working on the same problem and disputes over priority arise) since the evidence for patentability of the alleged invention will be clear-cut and less open to debate. In other words, it is highly probable that cases of pharmaceutical opposition will only occur with at least one party to the dispute (probably the opposer) being the holder of an important patented invention.

If so, then most pharmaceutical patents are held to be of little worth

Table 6.4 Some principal companies' patent and opposition activity (Sections 14 and 33), 1950–65

Firm	*Patents taken out*	*Oppositions begun*	*Oppositions defended*	*Defence as % of patents*
AMERICAN				
Abbot	249	6	2	0.8
Armour	165	1	1	0.6
Bristol	59	5	7	12.0
Cyanamid	788	23	13	1.7
Lilly	149	5	6	4.3
Merck	850	43	42	4.9
Miles	59	2	6	10.0
Ortho	46	1	1	2.2
Parke Davis	296	11	11	3.7
Pfizer	457	28	23	4.9
Riker	13	5	3	23.0
Robins	13	1	0	0
Searle	138	1	5	3.6
SKF	203	2	4	2.0
Squibb	266	0	8	3.0
Syntex	188	11	10	5.3
Upjohn	884	24	27	3.0
Warner	56	1	1	0.5
Winthrop	160	9	4	2.5
Wyeth	90	8	1	1.1
Total American	5129	187	175	3.4
BRITISH				
Beecham	137	11	10	7.3
Boots	134	4	4	3.0
BDH	125	10	10	8.0
Crookes	17	1	0	0
Fisons	59	9	0	0
Glaxo	234	13	12	5.1
Nicholas	46	2	5	10.8
Reckitt	26	0	4	15.2
Smith & Nephew	102	4	1	1.0
Vitamins	45	0	3	6.7
Wellcome	329	6	7	2.1
Total British	1254	60	56	4.5

Table 6.4 (continued)

Firm	*Patents taken out*	*Oppositions begun*	*Oppositions defended*	*Defence as % of patents*
EUROPEAN				
Ciba	1610	16	16	1.0
Geigy	724	5	1	0.1
Sandoz	281	10	7	2.5
Roche	815	9	12	1.5
Wander	61	1	1	1.6
Hoescht	681	0	7	1.0
Boehringer	109	4	7	6.4
Lepetit	152	2	10	6.6
Rhone Poulenc	679	20	7	1.0
Carlo Erba	17	0	1	5.9
Roussell Uclaf	360	4	5	1.4
Organon	101	4	4	4.0
Astra	28	4	2	7.1
Total European	5618	79	80	1.4
Grand total	12001	326	321	—
Average overall	—	—	—	2.6

Source: Author

since (*a*) they can be so readily 'patented around' by competitors, and (*b*) the patentees in turn will suffer little commercial damage from such activity. 'Important' patents, however, are just as easily 'patented around'; but in this case the potential commercial damage could be large, since a large technical advance will have resulted in a correspondingly large sector of the market being captured by the innovator. The hypothesis is that it is patents of this nature which are defended most assiduously by invoking opposition proceedings against others. The hypothesis is strengthened by the well-known fact that those who wish to compete on price, by applying for licences under Section 41, restrict their applications to the major innovations, obviously in the well-founded belief that market potential is markedly greater with such products.

4 Evaluation

(a) On the patent system's rationale

An R & D project is by definition a unique act, with no previous history of performance to indicate the probability levels of any particular set of outcomes. This implicit uncertainty in R & D, and in innovation itself, where market entry is with an untried product and reactions from competitors are unknown, renders it essential that those providing capital for R & D and innovation be awarded a higher than normal return to induce their investment.

If the innovation is successful, the speed with which it can be copied, of especial relevance in pharmaceuticals,* might soon reduce profit levels and prices to 'normal' and marginal cost levels respectively. Capital providers would consequently cease to invest in innovation with its associated risk and very brief period of abnormal rewards, when riskless, normal returns are available elsewhere.

This logic, plus possibly the argument of disclosure, is the prime reason for granting patent protection in pharmaceuticals.

(b) On the encouragement of minor innovations

Criticism of patents for pharmaceuticals comes from economists such as Henry Steele, who suggests that the industry could become perfectly competitive if, among other things, patenting was abolished.[10] He argues that industry R & D has not been successful, has produced mere substitutes and has not contributed to corporate growth. If this were true, then no doubt a strong case could be made for his initial contention. The latter statement, however, is not reconcileable with the facts of pharmacological history; and the advent of Steele's perfect competition would more than probably be accompanied by a dwindling of innovative activity. Steele's extreme position, however, has been encouraged by the unassailable fact that most patented inventions are run-of-the-mill by nature.

This is indicated by the vast difference in numbers between major drug discoveries and patents.† It also helps explain the low level of opposition activity under Sections 14 and 33. Firms with patent cover over minor technical advances will feel little danger of loss to other patentees with similar minor advances or technical differences. Only the

*In 1962 Merck were prepared to pay up to £10,000 to regain control of a stolen 'flow-sheet' of their own recently discovered highly research-intensive product 'Aldomet', and thus prevent it from falling into rivals' hands. See P. Hamilton, *Espionage and Subversion in an Industrial Society*, p. 51.

†In his 1974 submission of evidence to Senator Edward Kennedy's sub-committee investigating the US drug industry, Dr. Robert Ariès of Paris pointed out that in 1972 of the 1500 patents registered internationally – in two countries other than the country of origin – only 45 were genuine new drugs.

few major steps forward, with correspondingly high degrees of market success, need seriously fear the competition of later innovations. They have far more to lose.

This would appear, at first sight, to provide good reasons for abolishing pharmaceutical patents for all but important discoveries. Apart from the obvious difficulty of defining what is 'important' there would appear to be little need to maintain an administrative structure to provide patent cover for minor advances if that patent cover is implicitly regarded as of little worth by patentees. Such a suggestion, however, ignores the process of pharmaceutical R & D itself. Almost as soon as a new chemical compound is discovered and synthesised, the firm concerned will commence the activity necessary to provide it with patent cover. The firm may wait until some pharmacological activity is shown to be possessed by the compound but probably will not delay patenting until longer-term testing is performed to show just precisely what biological properties are present and how great an advance the compound would represent over existing therapies.

Patent protection is consequently applied for by drug houses because the inventions they desire to protect *might* be important, but the protection is sought prior to the firm itself knowing exactly what the technical and commercial potential of its discovery is. Patent protection is regarded at least initially, as essential for all grades of technical advance. When the inventor discovers the true worth of the invention, at a date after patent protection is first sought, the value placed on patent cover will vary with the intrinsic value of the invention.

(c) A possible solution

One solution, rather than abolishing patents for ephemeral advance, is to establish a two-tier system on lines suggested by Markam:

> The system would provide for relatively long periods of protection for major technological breakthroughs, because they are of high value and involve uncertainty and large research costs. It would also provide for much shorter-term protection for inventive effort generally considered to be an integral part of dynamic competition, and production of incremental changes no one of which adds substantially to society's total stock of knowledge.[11]

In pharmaceutical R & D, serendipity still plays a part in what is essentially a random process. Long-term projects can yield minor advances while mere molecular roulette can throw up substantial improvements in therapy. Since, therefore, drug patentees frequently use the system prior to assessing the value of their invention themselves, it appears that the tiering process could not be commenced until after long-term trials, and possibly not until market launch itself.*

On the other hand, to remove a legalised monopoly (patent protection) held in low esteem by the monopolist (the patentee) in an industry where patent networks are unimportant and where cracking one patent appears to be sufficient in many cases to allow competition within a product monopoly – this would seem to be an exercise to bring about a state of affairs which already exists.

Patentees do little if anything to prevent technically competitive encroachment on minor patents; access to a host of minor patents is unnecessary to market a newly-discovered advance. In a word, while a two-tier system has much to recommend it in industries characterised by patent networks like electronics (since minor entry barring patents would then have very short lives), it would appear to be a needless move which would little alter competitive behaviour in drugs (since, although minor patents undoubtedly exist, they do not appear to provide additional protection to the major discoveries protected by their respective individual patents).

Abuse of patent monopoly by exploiting minor differentials probably has not occurred (since patentees place very little value on such patents and so excess profits, if any, apparently do not spring from this particular source). On the other hand, while product differentiation may not have been exploited in such a way as to result in inordinately high profits, it may well have resulted in unnecessarily

*Thus if all new medicines with apparently only minor advantages were kept off the market due to changes in patent provision, some very significant therapeutic advances would have been lost. One such example would have been hydroxychloroquine, which appeared when first introduced to offer only some slight reduction of side-effects as compared with the antimalarial chloroquine. Subsequent experience showed it to be in a different class from its chemical predecessor and it is now a widely prescribed therapy for rheumatoid arthritis. In addition, new medicines which do not represent major advances may often be introduced at lower prices than their predecessors, thus bringing economic advantages. Finally, important advantages which may be recognised by a general practitioner actually using the therapy may be discounted by the experts. An example here is ferrous gluconate for anaemia as compared to ferrous sulphate. Professors of therapeutics argued for many years that the gluconate was no better than the cheaper sulphate; however, they never heard the patients' complaints to the nursing staff about sickness and vomiting following the use of the sulphate.

high cost curves, including R & D costs.* If so, then any strategically interdependent minimax policies firms might have adopted towards R & D will be reinforced by the availability of patent protection. In so far as this is the case, then a two-tier patent system might encourage the realisation by businessmen that not all R & D expenditure results in equally valuable technical and commercial advances. The current award of sixteen years' protection† to all patentable advances may have the opposite result, no matter how unimpressive are the sales profiles of minor advances several months or years after the actual decision to undertake the R & D in question.

In such a situation the *ante hoc* knowledge that minor advances will receive only minor protection may be a more effective deterrent of 'unnecessary' R & D than *post hoc* low commercial returns, indicating the relative lack of need for protection in the first place.

It must be admitted, however, that the administrative problems of such a scheme might prove impracticably large. For example, who is to say that the duplicate of a major breakthrough arrived at by a different technical route is a minor advance or merits full-scale patent protection in its own right? Some judicial organ would be essential to balance the conflicting evidence which would be produced in such a situation.

In summary, a two-tier system may be an unnecessary innovation in an industry with no entry barring minor patent networks, and where the costs of installing such a system could be well in excess of the benefits to be gained by inhibiting the very small R & D outlays directed at obtaining minor advances.

*Given the oligopolistic nature of pharmaceutical competition firms may be unwilling to cut back their R & D expenditures in case rivals do not do so and so gain a competitive advantage through a resulting minor innovation which might otherwise have been matched. If so, then this behaviour exists in the face of historical records indicating frequent and widespread failure rates by minor innovations, but it may be encouraged by the provision of patent protection. Oligopolies then may not only be price 'sticky' as in conventional theory, but may also be R & D 'sticky', and that at high level.

†An extension to 20 years is expected if the Banks Committee recommendations are enacted.

7 Relationships with the State

1 Historical development

The size of the nation's drug bill has been a matter for debate since the NHS was first established.

Brian Abel-Smith and Richard Titmuss conducted an investigation of the factors accounting for the rise of pharmaceutical service expenditure between 1949 and 1953/4. This was carried out on behalf of the Guillebaud Committee, which reported in 1956.[1] They concluded that about one-third of the rise was due to increased drug consumption since the inception of the NHS, and a similar proportion to the introduction of new and expensive drugs, particularly antibiotics – a trend reflected by the increased prescribing of branded drugs. The remaining causes were not specified.

Despite these apparently innocuous conclusions criticism continued and a further government committee was set up, the Hinchcliffe Committee,[2] whose terms of reference specifically directed it to have:

> regard to the increase in the cost of prescriptions issued under the NHS, to investigate the factors contributing to this cost and to make recommendations.

Hinchcliffe examined the proportion of total NHS expenditure incurred by the pharmaceutical services and concluded that:

> these figures do not support the general belief that the cost of the pharmaceutical service is increasing at a much faster rate than that of other branches of the NHS or that it is absorbing an increasing share in the total cost of the Service.[3]

The Times attempted to close the debate by stating that 'the size of the drug bill in Britain is not a problem at all – however, the belief that it is one, is a problem'.[4]

The revelations of the Kefauver Committee[5] in the United States, however, prevented any diminishing of the ardour of the industry's critics. Kefauver selected individual products which showed a profit margin at selling price of more than 90 per cent over factory cost. These examples gave ample encouragement to critics.[6] Official unease continued and a further committee, the Sainsbury Committee, was set up and reported in 1967.

In its chapter on prices and profits the Committee's Report concluded that profit levels are 'in some cases much higher than can be considered reasonable'.[7] This statement was based on a study of the return on capital employed by pharmaceutical firms over the period 1963–5. Three companies were discovered to be earning at between 50 and 55 per cent profit, some 30 per cent more than the modal group of companies at 20–25 per cent.

Curiously, the Report made no mention whatever of the record of these companies in periods prior to 1963. One was the Beecham Group. This company, however, ran its pharmaceutical operations at a loss for the preceding sixteen years while the massive and world-renowned research effort of Professor Chain and his colleagues was being financed in Rome and in the Beecham Laboratories in England. This resulted in the isolation of the penicillin nucleus and in the stream of new semi-synthetic penicillin variants which is still emanating from this company. A 50 per cent profit in any one period is not in itself either reasonable or unreasonable. It must be looked at in the context of the activities of the company over time.

2 Invoking countervailing power

In spite of, or perhaps because of, subjective and poorly-based judgements such as the condemnation of firms like Beecham, government interference in the drugs market in order to protect the interests of the NHS has increased. When, for whatever reasons, the benefits of classical price competition are apparently unavailable, one means of promoting efficiency and discouraging waste is to invoke the Galbraithian concept of Countervailing Power. In pharmaceuticals the bifurcation of customer activity, with the NHS footing the bill and a multiplicity of prescribers choosing the items which go to make it up, implies that countervailing power can be exercised in either of these areas. Intervention can be either direct, by influencing the prices of products already being prescribed; or indirect, by influencing the pattern of prescribing away from highly-priced products towards cheaper equivalents.

3 Price control

Government price control in pharmaceuticals is embodied in the Voluntary Price Regulation Scheme (VPRS).

Originally established in 1957 to ensure 'fair and reasonable' prices for products in Cohen* category 'S', the VPRS has now been revised several times and applies more generally to all branded ethical products. The most recent version of the VPRS is the 1972 agreement negotiated between the Department and the ABPI.

Basically the VPRS provides a framework for negotiation between the Department and the Company marketing a medicine. All companies with NHS sales of over £¾ million must supply the Department with a standardised Annual Financial Return which gives details of sales, costs and capital employed in the previous year. (Smaller firms are required to provide copies of their audited accounts together with a sales breakdown.) The Department consequently has at its disposal during negotiations information on promotional levels and profitability. In the course of negotiations companies may be called upon to satisfy the Department on other matters, including transfer prices of materials supplied by affiliated companies, and the amount of overseas costs and capital to be taken into account in considering the firm's British business. If after reviewing the prices charged the Department is still in doubt as to their acceptability, it may apply one of two supplementary tests. The first involves comparison with prices in similar overseas markets: the second – for use where the first is not applicable – entails comparison with prices of other closely comparable products in the home market. (Price adjustments, however, can still be made by firms without reference to the Department if annual NHS sales of the product are less than £150,000, or £50,000 if the product accounts for over 10 per cent of the firm's total NHS sales.)

The OHE has estimated that during 1970 alone the cumulative effect of price reductions negotiated under the VPRS since 1965 resulted in a

*See below, p. 104.

total reduction of industry profits of £18 m. This is in the context of sales at manufacturers' prices of £170 m.

Whether or not exercise of Departmental monopsonistic power is desirable is debatable. There is, however, one area on which the VPRS, as currently constituted offends. No guidance is given as to what levels of profits or costs (such as promotion) should be considered 'reasonable'. The outcome of negotiations will therefore to some extent depend on the relative skills of the bargainers. Thus, companies may be treated differently according to their negotiating expertise. Of necessity this must lead to unpredictable, if not arbitrary, outcomes.

Such capriciousness is increased by the fact that negotiation is based on accounting returns which misstate profits and costs in those instances (the majority) where the firm is a foreign-owned subsidiary. Subsidiaries may produce proven profits, often with little in the way of fixed assets, use rented property and draw on the R & D of the parent in another country. Given that profitability is measured by return on capital then assets in the subsidiary's balance sheet are low and profitability correspondingly high; costs, which do not include R & D, are unrealistic; and so on. Alternatively, the subsidiary may be charged a transfer price above the going market rate for raw materials. This will make a contribution to overall company costs, will reduce subsidiary profits and UK tax liability. Such difficulties lessen in time if a subsidiary becomes relatively autonomous but are never eliminated. Local decisions only make sense in the international setting, viewed from the parent's head office and based on overall trading accounts.

Problems of measurement and arbitrariness, aside from considerations of 'fairness', must affect management forecasting, planning and so decision making. Businessmen make investment decisions (which include R & D expenditure) most readily in conditions of certainty. To the extent that the VPRS has increased uncertainty about future prices and profits in pharmaceuticals then investment and R & D decisions may be adversely effected.

4 Influencing prescribing patterns

If prescribing habits can be nudged away from expensive products, then price reductions may occur in an attempt to regain customer, namely government, favour. Looked at in this way, the influencing of prescribing patterns can be regarded as indirect price control. The prescribing of products considered 'undesirable' for other reasons can also be influenced.

The principle of qualitatively classifying the products of the industry in an attempt to control prescribing is as old as the NHS. In 1949 the Joint Committee on Prescribing was set up to:

> Consider and report from time to time whether it is desirable and practicable to resist or discourage the prescribing by practitioners . . . of
>
> 1. drugs and medicines of doubtful value or unethical character;
> 2. unnecessarily expensive brands of standard drugs.

The Committee defined six classifications of drugs of varying degrees of desirability. By 1953 the Committee had classified all then available drugs and recommended the setting up of a smaller standing committee to add new products as they became available.

The Standing Joint Committee on the Classification of Proprietary Preparations (the Cohen Committee) was set up in 1954. Basically, the classification system permitted doctors freedom of prescription (categories 'N' and 'P') of non-standard drugs for which there was evidence of therapeutic value. Prescribing of drugs of unproven value was discouraged (categories 'O' and 'H'), alone or in combination with approved drugs. Under category 'S' the prescribing of branded equivalents of standard drugs, of other combinations, or of medicines only slightly varying from standard was also discouraged. 'Standard' meant those drugs listed in publications such as the *British National Formulary* (BNF).

'Discouragement' took two main forms. The Committee agreed that there should be 'no absolute restrictions' on the doctor's freedom to prescribe for his individual patient's needs but that if his overall cost of prescribing was being investigated then he might be called on to justify his prescriptions in categories 'O', 'H' and 'S'. Further, category 'S' drugs should only be prescribable if a price had been agreed on for the product between the Ministry and the manufacturer. To apply this 'discouragement' the VPRS was developed. Embodied in the doctor's terms of employment are conditions stipulating that remuneration may be withheld if excessively costly prescribing is proved. Each GP receives an annual statement showing his prescription costs, the average for his area and for the country. If his are substantially above average he may receive a visit from a Regional Medical Officer who will discuss his prescribing with him. (In England and Wales 3000 such visits were paid in 1972.)[8] If his costs are deemed excessive the case may be referred to the Local Medical Committee who are empowered to withhold remuneration. Only one such reference made in 1972, and the doctor had £50 withheld from his salary.

In 1964 the Cohen Committee was wound up and reconstituted under the chairmanship of Professor MacGregor. This reconstruction was brought about by the removal of some of Cohen's functions to the newly-established Committee on Safety of Drugs and by the growing feeling that the Cohen classifications were somewhat confusing.

The MacGregor Committee was set up with the following terms of reference:

> To advise on the classification of proprietary pharmaceutical preparations with the object of helping doctors to decide which should be used in the treatment of their patients, and to identify these preparations the prescribing of which appears to call for special justification.

In 1965 the Committee published its system of classification. The Committee recommended freedom of prescription for its first four categories and discouragement for its last two. Briefly, MacGregor categories M and A1 contained standard drugs, or those non-standard drugs with little or no therapeutic difference from standard equivalents. Categories A2 and A3 contained preparations which could be recommended for use but which were considered unacceptable due to lack of proven efficacy or excess toxicity.

The public face of the Committee was its periodical publication *Proplist* which contained details of all the preparations classified. *Proplist* was circulated to each doctor. (Other semi-official attempts at moulding prescribing patterns are embodied in the periodical *Prescribers' Journal*, issued free of charge to all doctors by the Department of Health. It contains articles about new and existing medicines in clinical use. Editorial policy is determined by an independent panel of clinicians and academics.)

Whether or not MacGregor had much of an effect on prescribing is an open question. 'Doctrinaire' was a term frequently used of the Committee's attitudes, particularly towards combination products. The ABPI on requesting pointers to the Committee's overall policy received little satisfaction in reply. 'Apart from indicating certain combinations of drugs which it considers not good medical practice to prescribe, the Committee does not feel it possible to give more precise guidance.'[9]

This acrimony may not have been noticed at the level of the prescriber but the inconsistency of *Proplist* and its failure on occasion to agree with even its semi-official stable-mate, *Prescribers' Journal*, must have added to confusion and lessened the effect of both on prescribing patterns. For example, the removal of Organon's 'Dilavase' from category B to A between the April and October 1967 issues of *Proplist* and a similar classification change of Moore's 'Isobrovon Tablets' between October and December 1967 smack more of quick-fire Committee decisions following successful lobbying by the firms than they do of judgements made within objective clear-cut guidelines. Similarly the Boots' combination product 'Abicol' was categorised B by *Proplist* in April 1968, yet, in the very same month *Prescribers' Journal* gave it the stamp of approval[10] and went on to say that 'drug combinations, whether they are administrated in the same tablet or separately, deserve more careful study than they have received in the past'.[11]

To the observer, it would appear that the knowledge to lay down guidelines for choice is not yet sufficiently available to preclude subjective judgements. Propagating the views of one school of thought in such a situation may not be appropriate. The dangers of such uniformity were succinctly put by *The Economist*: 'If anyone disputes this let him ask himself why a middle-class generation, born between the wars, has grown up without its tonsils or its foreskin.'[12]

This lesson has apparently been learned. *Proplist* and the Committee responsible for its publication were stood down in 1968. By 1972, however, the Committee on Safety of Medicines (see below) was contemplating assuming to itself an educative role. The Annual Report of the Chief Medical Officer to the Department of Health stated that the Committee had reviewed its policy in relation to efficacy:

> As a result it concluded that there was a need for a change in its attitude to harmless products of doubtful efficacy. Hitherto the Committee had considered that the Medicines Act should not be used to deny the public the use of products which presented no hazards. In the future the Committee will require the application for such a product to be supported by some evidence of efficacy before advising that a product licence should be granted.*

*Since this was written it has been decided to review the efficacy of the existing 36,000 products which have been given licences of right. Some of these products have been on the market for 50 years or longer and were – and often still are – considered mightily efficacious by doctors and patients; after all, a placebo is often found to be effective. Will there be a fuss when a favourite potion is withdrawn on the grounds that the experts find it useless? It is strange, too, that with medicines now so rigorously scrutinised little or no attention is paid to the effects of

5 Control of quality and safety

The tragic, although at the time unpredictable, thalidomide catastrophe in 1963 was a major factor leading to the establishment *of the Committee on Safety of Drugs, under the chairmanship* of Sir Derrick Dunlop (since 1968, the Committee on Safety of Medicines, chaired by Professor Scowen).

Prior to this Britain, in common with most other nations, had laws for narcotics, and also for certain ethical drugs covered by the poisons rules, the Therapeutic Substances Act, and the Dangerous Drugs Act. The registration formalities under these Acts were, however, relatively simple. The control procedure exercised by the Ministry of Health did not begin until *after* the product was launched on the market and in any event amounted only to a referral to the Cohen Committee for classification.

Since the implementation of the Medicines Act 1968, the Secretary of State for Social Services has had the right to grant or withhold licences governing the marketing, manufacture and importation of any medical product. The Department of Health's Inspectorate has the right to establish, by physical visit, whether or not the premises, personnel and manufacturing techniques of an applicant firm are adequate.

With regard to new products the Secretary, as licensing authority, uses the advice of the Scowen Committee as to whether or not a licence be granted or refused.

The first stage in the registration procedure for a new drug comes prior to external clinical trial. A clinical trial certificate is only granted on proof of satisfactory bio-assay results and/or initial clinical trial success. A product licence to market a new drug is only recommended by the Committee on submission of satisfactory clinical trial results. Table 7.1 gives the outcome of such applications made during 1972.

As far as these procedures on clinical trials and new product introductions are concerned, the Scowen Committee functions very little differently from its predecessor, Dunlop. The main difference is

---

surgery. Yet the mortality from an operation is much higher than is officially attributed to drugs. Professor Bunker has estimated that the 2 million operations performed in Great Britain in a year yield 20–30,000 deaths as a result of surgery, or the anaesthetic itself. Nor is surgery by any means always life-saving. Most of it is directed towards the relief of disability, discomfort and disfigurement, and there are wide discrepancies between one country and another in the number of discretionary, as distinct from emergency operations. But who protects us from the over-zealous surgeon? And who assesses the efficacy of surgery? (John Bunker, 'Risks and Benefits of Surgery' in *Benefits and Risk in Medical Care*, David Taylor (editor), OHE, 1975.)

Table 7.1 Details of applications referred to the Committee on Safety of Medicines, 1972

	Clinical trial certificates	*Product licences*	*Totals*
Issue or grant advised			
(i) without modification	102	336	438
(ii) subject to modification following discussions	—	1	1
Extension requested and advised	8	9	17
Refusal advised	3	2	5
Withdrawn	5	14	19
In hand			
(i) modification proposed	1	1	2
(ii) refusal proposed	8	21	29
Deferred by the Committee for further information	26	22	48
Totals	153	406	559

Source: Annual Report of the Chief Medical Officer of the Department of Health and Social Security, 1972 (HMSO) p. 163.

that submissions to the Scowen Committee are obligatory and its judgements have the sanction of the licensing law. The Dunlop Committee relied on voluntary collaboration by pharmaceutical firms.

The third function of the Committee is post-marketing surveillance of all medicines, old and new. The Committee examines reports voluntarily submitted by practitioners on adverse reactions of patients to medicines. If these reports are significant all prescribers may be informed of the reaction in question. (In 1972, 3638 such notifications were received from GPs but no special warnings were issued as a result.)

Finally, to ensure that all prescribers are aware of the contra-indications of all medicines the Medicines Act lays down that each must receive a Data Sheet from the manufacturer at intervals no greater than 15 months. The ABPI has prepared a joint compendium of most Data Sheets to facilitate their use by prescribers. Promotional claims must then fall within the boundaries set by the Data Sheet.

The Act lays down the format and type size for data sheet entries and requires information to be given on the uses of the medicines, dosage, precautions and warnings on side-effects, package quantities and other data.

6 Another view

Sir Derrick Dunlop has remarked that doctors 'have the absolute power to determine the sales of ethical drugs, and if our wishes are expressed on our prescription pads they will be heeded'. The Department of Health, realising this, has tried to encourage the profession to use this power.

Doctors are frequently circularised with histograms showing the comparative prices of therapeutic substitutes in an attempt to increase the profession's price-consciousness. Financial encouragement, by way of salary increments, is given to the profession to attend refresher courses, including those on pharmacology and therapeutics. This is at least partly in the hope that more discriminating prescribing would result.

Despite these efforts it would appear that a fully effective, fully informed countervailing force has yet to be developed. Inglis[13] went as far as to say that 'the medical profession, then, can no longer be relied upon to protect the public'. The implication behind this statement is that the prescriber does not know sufficient about the range of choice facing him to be selective, nor does he have the motivation to remedy this state of affairs.

The lack of motivation is certainly indicated by an examination of the circulation figures of the non-profit-making *Drugs and Therapeutic Bulletin.* Published by the Consumers Association, it was first issued in 1962 and is published fortnightly. It provides consensus appraisals of new and existing drugs and gives comparative performance assessments. Despite the uniqueness of this service, by 1968 less than one doctor in ten had bothered to subscribe the necessary £3.30 per annum (chargeable for income tax purposes as a business expense).

If there is an unnecessary heterogeneity of products, then the power to alter the situation lies within the hands of the medical profession. The impact of the isolation effect, discussed above, and the outpacing of the profession's knowhow by pharmacological advance inhibits the exercise of this power. It is perhaps to this area, rather than to the industry's activities that public concern could be turned. (Having said this, one must remember that Chamberlinian hypothesis that increased knowledge of heterogeneous consumer needs can *increase* desire for product differentiation.)[14]

The alternative is increasing legislation and control with or without increased prescriber price and quality awareness. The British industry now has more controls that even before. This is making market entry

Table 7.2 Comparative introduction dates of selected American innovations, UK and USA

Product	*Manufacturer*	*UK*	*USA*
Lincocin	Upjohn	May 1964	January 1965
Tegopen	Bristol	October 1962	April 1965
Presate	Warner	May 1961	April 1965
Indocid	Merck	July 1964	July 1965
Ovulen	Searle	June 1964	May 1966
Brufen	Boots	November 1959	January 1975

Source: Private correspondence, M. Weber, Intercontinental Medical Statistics Ltd.

costlier and increasingly difficult for the smaller firm. In America, where stiffer legislation and its attendant bureaucratic obstacles of time and cost have been in existence for much of the sixties, Oliker concluded that the small firm had suffered a loss in competitive position due to its lack of facilities to comply with the regulations. The dominance and permanence of the large firms already in any one therapeutic market was consequently increased.[15]

Wyndham-Davies, studying the American legislation,[16] observed that a new drug takes two to three years to be cleared by the Food and Drug Administration's Safety of Drugs Section. This compares with the average processing period in Britain of three months. Davies blames this on the slow, inefficient operation of a vast and expensive bureacratic machine. The effect of this, apart from increasing costs, including those of sales foregone, is that the public is deprived of technical advances which it otherwise might have been enjoying. The situation is not so serious in Britain. Table 7.2 indicates much tardier introduction dates for recent advances by American firms in their domestic market compared with their UK introduction. A delay caused not by failure to perform the necessary clinical and animal testing, since Scowen demands satisfactory evidence of this before approving a product, but by the slow-moving wheels of FDA bureaucracy.

In the present state of pharmacological knowledge, even if the delays noted in Table 7.2 represented evidence of greater testing, it would not be proof of greater drug safety. Another thalidomide will not be avoided by more stringent testing than that already performed in industrial laboratories. Safety in use in animals does not guarantee safety in use in man. Until predictability of chemical action on human tissues is possible the use of a new drug for the first time on a human being will be fraught with potential danger.* The failure of even extensive clinical trials to mirror a drug's behaviour in the population at large (as for example with the disappointed hopes of rheumatologists in the original cortisone) further entails, as Dr Cahal, the full-time head of the Dunlop committee, emphasised, that 'the only way to ensure that drug-induced embryopathies do not occur is not to give drugs to women of child-bearing age'.[17] There is a point after which no amount of prior testing can remove from the prescriber his ultimate responsibility for the safety of his patient.

Laurence emphasises this responsibility in a standard textbook in British medical schools:

> Before treating any patient with drugs the doctor should have made up his mind on five points:
>
> 1. Whether he should interfere with the patient at all, and if so,
> 2. What alteration in the patient's condition he hopes to achieve.
> 3. That the drug he intends to use is capable of bringing this about.
> 4. What other effects the drug may have and whether they may be harmful.
> 5. Whether the likelihood of benefit, and its importance, outweighs the likelihood of damage, and its importance.

Laurence succinctly concludes with the advice that 'if in doubt whether or not to give a drug, don't'.[18] The readiness of GPs to reach for their prescription pads, possibly occasioned by pressure of patients and the need to 'clear the surgery', suggests that this advice is but little heeded.

> . . . as long as drugs are voluntarily taken by healthy young women who do not need them, the risk of damaging their babies will be something that many doctors will feel they deliberately bring on themselves. What, then, is the real liability of the manufacturer or the doctor or the state? This is the moral aspect that many people have shown a remarkable reluctance to discuss.[19]

*Professor Alistair MacGregor in his Morris Block Lecture delivered in Glasgow in 1963 stated that it is 'a delusion that effective tests can be developed which can protect the public . . . No test at all has yet been devised in animal species that can with certainty predict such an action [tetragenic effects].' MacGregor cited the rather startling examples of species variability in that only six times the normal dosage of aspirin for rheumatics is required to produce a deformed rat foetus, and contrariwise it requires seventy-five times the normal dosage of thalidomide before rabbit malformation results.

In conclusion, it is worth considering the view that it might be to society's net advantage if attempts to control the market for pharmaceuticals were directed at the demand rather than the supply component. While the industry may be accused of competitive practices resulting in resource misallocation, there is little to indicate that it is operating in a technically inefficient manner in either the production, marketing or R & D functions. The medical profession on the other hand, in its capacity as a purchaser, is demonstrably technically inefficient.* It has limited price consciousness and it is uncertain what, if any, criteria to use to gauge the comparative efficacy of competing products. The removal of these imperfections from the demand component might do more to improve the economic efficiency of operation of the pharmaceutical market than state interference on the supply side.

*This statement is not restricted to prescribing habits. Twenty-five per cent of hospital patients have no therapeutic or diagnostic need to be there. The Sheffield Regional Board was less well-endowed than that of Oxford on all of thirty-one indices of health provision (e.g. GPs, consultants, and hospital beds *per capita*) with no apparent detriment in mortality or morbidity. Was Sheffield deprived or simply more efficient? (Cited from M. H. Cooper, 'Rationing and Financing Health Care Resources' in *Management in the Social and Safety Services*, edited by W. Duncan Reekie and N. C. Hunt, 1974.)

8 Current Areas of Controversy

1 Market structure

The debate which surrounds the topic of market structure is intimately connected with the relationship between Research and Development and size of firm. The proposed merger between Beecham and Glaxo was turned down by the Monopolies Commission primarily because of the adverse effects it might have on pharmaceutical R & D in the United Kingdom.

The controversy has two main facets. First, whether or not larger firms perform proportionately more R & D than smaller. Second, whether or not larger R & D efforts produce proportionately more innovations.

R & D is an absolutely expensive activity and it is presumed that firms must be of some minimum size in order to undertake a meaningful effort. The NEDO study of the industry suggested that in 1970 terms the smallest R & D effort, based on at least three projects, would cost a minimum of £½ million. Possibly a budget of nearer £2 million is required in order to support a full range of skills and facilities and to provide some insurance against failure. Those who argue that larger firms conduct proportionately more R & D do so on the bases that larger firms (*a*) have greater resources and (*b*) have a greater degree of market power which can be used to generate an absolutely higher level of profits from any resulting innovation. This is a familiar argument and has been with us at least since Schumpeter first wrote of the 'Perennial Gate of Creative Destruction'.[1] Disagreement arises not over the need to have some degree of size and market power to encourage R & D activity, but over whether or not an increase in market power and size above such a threshold would result in a relatively complacent large firm whose urge to engage in the risks of innovative activity would be relatively less. For example, referring to the Beecham–Glaxo merger proposal the Monopolies Commission wrote:

> Beecham's research interests are relatively narrow, as is also the range of drugs which it sells. The prosperity of such a company is . . . vulnerable . . . (and it has) in consequence, a strong incentive to remedy its potential weakness by broadening the scope of its research. Should Beecham acquire Glaxo . . . the resulting company would be much less vulnerable . . . and some of the research which Beecham might otherwise have done . . . might not be undertaken.[2]

The second facet of the controversy, whether larger R & D efforts are more productive, is, of course, merely a restatement, in the R & D situation, of the question as to when, if at all, scale economies are exhausted. The *a priori* case for and against the existence of diseconomies of scale in R & D is even more indefinable than in the manufacturing area. R & D productivity depends to a considerable extent on individual creativity. Jewkes[3] and his associates have shown that inventive creativity is scattered fairly evenly across the size distribution of organisations. When an invention moves into the stage of applied research and development, however, it is often argued that there is then more scope for the economic advantages of size to result in an overall reduction in unit costs.

A number of empirical studies have been published in recent years which have examined these areas of dispute. Tables 8.1 and 8.2 summarise the results obtained. Only one study, and that inconclusively, suggests that total R & D effort might increase if the industry were composed of fewer and larger firms. The investigations carried out by Grabowski, Mansfield, this author and the Monopolies Commission all arrive at broadly the same conclusion: the largest pharmaceutical firms, while possibly the biggest absolute performers of R & D, are not the most research-intensive firms.

The studies reported in Table 8.2 differed in their objectives, in their statistical methodology, and in their measures of innovative output. A wholly satisfactory yardstick of innovation has yet to be devised. However, the range of indices employed in Table 8.2 does cover most of the parameters generally thought of as indicators of the value of a new medicine to society. Despite the employment of so many different measures of R & D success the studies by Comanor, Grabowski, the

Table 8.1 Summary of results of studies relating size of firm to R & D efforts

Study	*Index of firm size*	*Index of R & D effort*	*Conclusions*
Grabowski[4]	Sales	R & D expenditure	Research intensity initially increases with firm size, but declines thereafter.
Mansfield[5]	Sales	R & D expenditure	R & D expenditure does not increase more than proportionately with firm size.
Monopolies Commission[6]	Sales	R & D expenditure	The relationship is non-linear. Intensity reaches a maximum below maximum firm size.
Reekie[7]	Sales	R & D expenditure	The relationship is non-linear. Intensity reaches a maximum below maximum firm size.
Schwartzman[8]	Sales	R & D employment (exclusive of auxiliary staff).	R & D effort increases less than proportionately with firm size if a linear logarithmic equation is used. The results are reversed if a quadratic equation is tested.

Monopolies Commission, this author, and by Schnee all fall into a common pattern. All suggest the presence of diseconomies of scale in pharmaceutical R & D.

Angilley, however, discovered constant returns to scale. And Schwartzman, reproducing (with certain statistical differences) most of the previous studies, came to the very opposite conclusion, that economies of scale *are* important.

How can these differences be reconciled? If one ignores the intricacies and technicalities of econometric debate, then the most obvious differences between Angilley and Schwartzman and the earlier studies is in the time periods which the two groups cover. The Angilley and Schwartzman studies are restricted to the second half of the 1960s.

Table 8.2 Summary of results of studies relating size of R & D effort to innovative output

Study	*Index of R & D effort*	*Index of R & D output*	*Period covered by study*	*Conclusions*
Angilley[10]	R & D Expenditure	New compounds (a) weighted by market success (b) weighted by degree of therapeutic advance	1958–70	'No strong deviation from constant returns to scale exists'
Comanor[9]	Professional research personnel	First 24 months sales of new single entities	1955–60	'Substantial diseconomies of scale in R & D encountered even by moderately sized firms'
Grabowski[4]	Professional research personnel	Patents	1959–62	Large firms do not necessarily have higher research productivity than smaller
Monopolies Commission[6]	Size of firm gauged by sales	Major pharmaceutical innovations	1950–71	Largest firms were responsible for a disproportionately small number of innovations

Reekie[7]	R & D expenditure	Patents	1959–66	Firms below the largest size were not only the most research intensive but also among the most successful
Schnee[11]	Size of firm gauged by sales	Major innovations, with or without medical or economic weights	1935–62	'The firms that have contributed the most innovations relative to their size are not the largest firms, but somewhat smaller ones'
Schwartzmann[8]	R & D employment (exclusive of auxiliary staff)	(a) New entities	1965–70	'Economies of scale are large'
		(b) New entities weighted by 1972 sales		'Economies of scale are large'
		(c) weighted by Novelty		'Large and increasing economies of scale'
		(d) Weighted by Medical Importance		'Large and increasing economies of scale'
		(e) Weighted by the number of prescriptions issued in 1971		'Large and increasing economies of scale'
		(f) Patents	1968–70	'Large economies of scale'

The others are predominantly or exclusively dependent on data relating to years prior to this period.

This may be significant and may indicate changing circumstances in pharmaceutical R & D. It has already been pointed out that the real costs of R & D are rising. This was attributable to two factors. The remaining unconquered disease areas provide relatively difficult technological problems. Second, the costs of meeting the requirements for new drug registration, both in the UK and overseas, have risen dramatically. Both are phenomena of the 1960s. They may be responsible for the apparent contradictions evident in Tables 8.1 and 8.2. Certainly a dogmatic stance cannot be taken with regard to the presence or absence of scale economies in R & D.

Finally, there is the more general issue that success in pharmaceutical research depends primarily on the ability to generate promising novel ideas. Given the serendipitous nature of much pharmaceutical R & D it would seem from a nationalistic viewpoint that the current small number of British-owned research centres in the UK should not be further reduced. Such a reduction might merely lead to fewer different ideas being pursued in any given field of common interest and so impair the British-owned industry's overall prospects of success in finding and developing new products.

2 Profits and prices

The DTI price index reveals that the prices of pharmaceutical chemicals and preparations in 1972 were only 7.7 per cent higher than in 1963 (Table 8.3). By contrast the prices of all manufactured products rose by an average of 45 per cent over the same period.

Table 8.3 Manufacturer's price index numbers (1963 = 100)

Year	*Pharmaceutical chemicals and preparations*	*Year*	*Pharmaceutical chemicals and preparations*
1964	99.0	1968	94.7
1965	97.3	1969	94.7
1966	94.4	1970	97.4
1967	95.4	1971	102.6
		1972	107.7

Source: Department of Trade and Industry.

There is an apparent paradox in that prices have been falling for much of the last decade while the cost of pharmaceuticals to the NHS has been (in money terms) continuously rising. This is partly due to rising distribution and dispensing costs and partly to changing prescribing patterns which are not reflected in the make-up of the index. As pharmacological knowledge widens and new medicines are introduced which are more effective, less toxic, or have fewer side-effects than their predecessors then doctors will take advantage of these improved remedies. New medicines, like new products in many markets, tend to be introduced at a relatively high price in order to cover the relatively high costs of innovation. As time passes the prices tend to be progressively lowered until they are closer to marginal production cost.

With regard to profitability in the industry the NEDO study amplified and updated much of Sainsbury's information. In a survey of 110 drug firms the average return on capital was found to be 29.8 per cent in the period 1960–2, and for 1967–9, 25.6 per cent. Table 8.4 shows the year-by-year pattern of profits from 1960 to 1969 as a percentage of sales. Two main questions are raised by profitability figures. First, are they fair and reasonable? Second, to what extent does the continued performance of R & D depend on continued and high levels of profit?

The two points are closely related. The Sainsbury Report spelt out the problem:

> There would be little inducement for firms to take on a specially high risk in searching for a particular medicine which may be eagerly desired in medical practice if there were to be no possibility of unusual profit, and a high probability of failure after considerable costs had been incurred. In such circumstances a 'normal' return on

Table 8.4 110 Pharmaceutical firms: profit levels 1960–9

Year	*Profit (before tax) on sales %*	*Year*	*Profit (before tax) on sales %*
1960	18.7	1965	16.0
1961	21.1	1966	15.1
1962	19.2	1967	13.3
1963	17.7	1968	14.3
1964	18.2	1969	14.1

Source: NEDO, op. cit., p. 31.

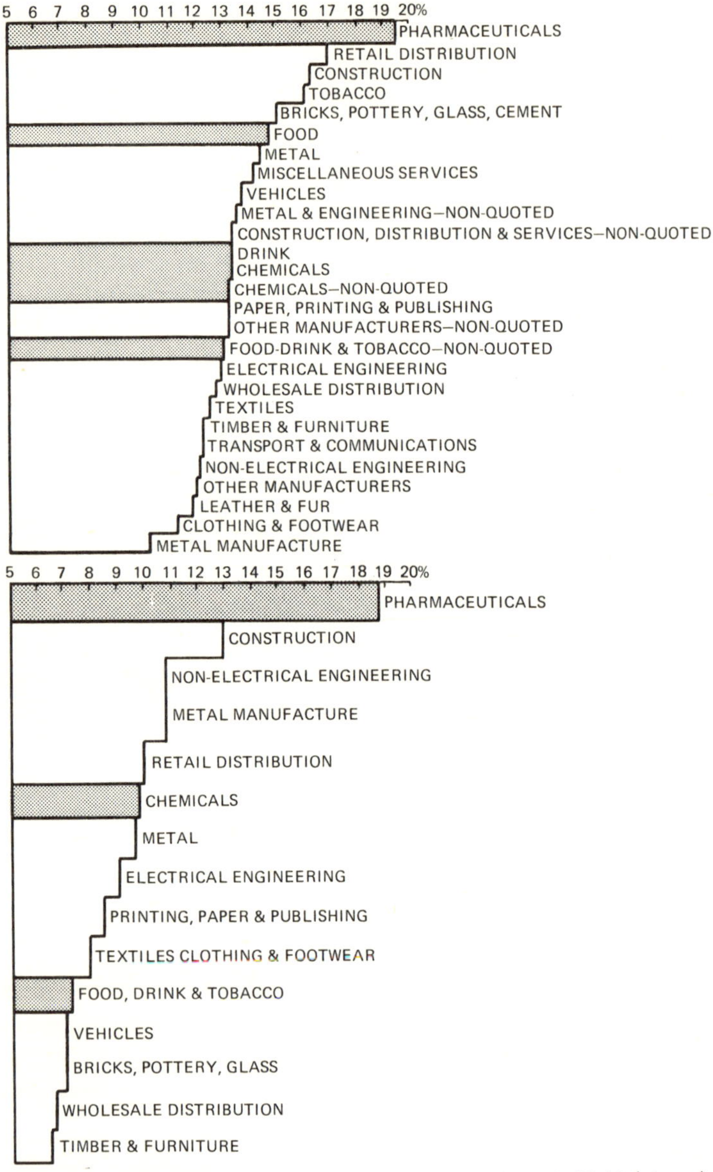

Fig. 8.1 UK Industry: return on capital employed, 1965 (above) and risk, 1963–5 (below)

Source: Merrett-Cyriax Associates, *Profitability in the Pharmaceutical Industry* (London, 1968).

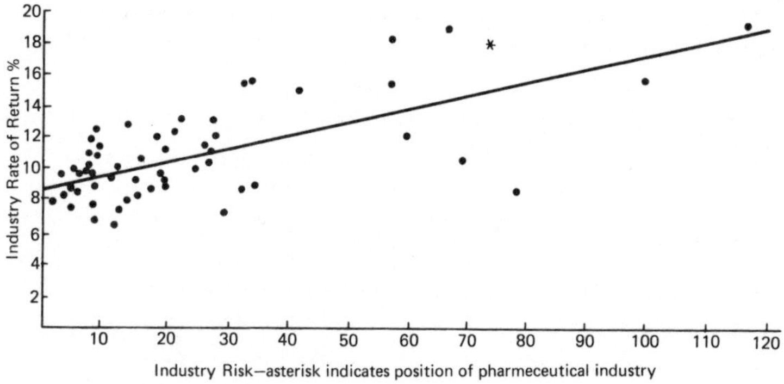

Fig. 8.2 Rates of return and risk factors in US industry

Source: Conrad and Plotkin, *Risk and Rates of Return in US Industry* (New York: Arthur D. Little, 1967).

> the sum risked would provide little inducement for a firm with safer alternative uses for its money to undertake research with higher risks.[12]

After making this point the Report went on to conclude that some profit levels in the industry were higher than 'reasonable'.* It is hard to discover a rationale for this conclusion, given that no attempt was made in the Report either to assess 'risk', or to relate pharmaceutical profitability with returns on capital in comparable industries. Figs. 8.1 and 8.2 summarise the results of two studies, one British and one American, which carried out such inter-industry, risk/profitability comparisons.

Both used, as indices of risk, measures of the dispersion of profitability between the most and the least profitable firms in an industrial grouping. That is, if industrial profitability covered a wide spread, there was more chance of a company falling substantially below the average return (and, of course, on the other hand of doing substantially better than the average). In these circumstances an entrant to the industry can be less certain of what return it is likely to achieve than it would be in an industry where all companies achieve more or less the same level of profitability. By this criterion the drug industry was the riskiest of the industries studied in Fig. 8.1. Fig. 8.2 displays a good correlation between high profitability and high risk, and the drug

*One of the firms concerned was the Beecham Group. See p. 101 above.

industry fits well into the overall pattern, having very much the level of profitability to be expected for an industry in its position on the risk scale.

More recent critics have been no less subjective than the Sainsbury Committee. The Monopolies Commission pronounced that the profits made by Roche Products Ltd were 'quite unjustified' and 'manifestly too high'.[13] These profit levels were alleged to be the direct result of 'excessive prices charged'.[14] This conclusion was arrived at while conceding that the two main Roche medicines, 'Librium' and 'Valium', had dosage costs 'amongst the lowest when compared with competitive products'. The Commission then claimed that there was a 'virtual absence of price competition'. Licences granted under Section 41 to Berk which resulted in a 36 per cent 'Valium' price reduction in six months were dismissed by the Commission not as competitive reaction, but '(misjudgment of) the strength of the competition'.[15] Roche held 60 per cent of the tranquilliser market with the products in question. The Commission discounted, with no explanation, Roche's argument that it held only 13 per cent of the relevant market. This was based on the high cross-elasticity of demand between tranquillisers and other groupings such as barbiturates. As a consequence of its prices policy Roche spent 'too much' on research, 15 per cent of total sales, compared with the industry average of around 10 per cent. It is difficult to know what is wrong with research; in any event, statistically some figures must always be above, and some below, an average. Roche was ordered to substantially reduce its 1970 prices. Roche is suing the British government for loss of earnings on the grounds that the orders were invalid. In such an absence of any serious economic study of the industry and markets in which Roche was operating then any pronouncement on 'fairness' and 'reasonableness' must suffer since, to cite Polanyi, 'it has no generally accepted meaning'.[16]

Michael Cooper carried out a comparison of the general level of prices of medicines in the UK and in other countries on behalf of NEDO in 1972. While a price comparison may not alone be sufficient to indicate whether or not prices and profits are monopolistically high, it can go some way to reducing subjectivity in criticism.

The main conclusion was that the UK market, which had been relatively low priced in 1964, was one of the lowest priced in 1970 (Table 8.5). The study also showed that the UK had experienced a relatively low growth of per capita expenditure on medicine between 1964 and 1969 – 54 per cent compared with a range of 98–146 per

Table 8.5 Total cost of buying comparable packs of those of the leading 20 UK products available in both the UK and each foreign market, January 1970

Country	*Cost in UK* £	*Cost in foreign market* £
Belgium	9.51	11.16
Finland	11.75	11.44
France	5.76	6.32
Germany	6.48	6.08
Italy	6.64	7.22
Japan	9.57	39.10
Japan (without product 1)	6.12	15.80
Spain	5.38	5.28
Turkey	8.26	10.30

Note: Chemist buying prices in decimal sterling.

Source: International Price Comparison (NEDO, 1972).

cent for the four other countries (France, W. Germany, Italy and Spain) for which information was available.

NEDO concluded that the relatively low prices and low growth of per capita expenditure on medicines in the UK may have arisen partly from competitive and market factors, but that they were probably also partly due to the countervailing power of the VPRS.

Prices and profitability have been displaying a declining trend (Tables 8.3 and 8.4). What implications does this have for future investment in R & D? A declining rate of return implies that firms will seek more profitable outlets for funds than pharmaceutical R & D. Yet large British drug firms have recently been announcing increases, not reductions, in their real (as opposed to monetary) levels of expenditure.*

This apparent paradox is partly resolved by Table 8.6. Here Kenneth Smith shows that the growth rate of pharmaceutical profits has been slowing down since the period 1966–7. On the other hand, *relative* to manufacturing industry as a whole, to chemicals or to the food, drink and tobacco industry, pharmaceuticals remain an attractive investment location.

*ICI intend to invest £100–£150 m in drug R & D between 1973 and 1982. Annual spending reaches over £8 m in 1974 (*Daily Telegraph*, 15 October 1973).

Table 8.6 Annual percentage changes in gross profits (industry totals)

Year	*Total manufacturing*	*Chemicals and allied*	*Food, drink and tobacco*	*Pharmaceuticals*
1965–6	–5.4	5.8	2.3	10.0
1966–7	2.2	8.4	4.0	22.0
1967–8	13.9	12.3	5.6	13.0
1968–9	–5.8	–2.5	–4.0	9.0

Source: Kenneth G. D. Smith, *Profitability, risk and investment in R & D* in G. Teeling-Smith (ed.), *The Pharmaceutical Industry and Society* (OHE, 1973).

Whether or not the incentive to invest in R & D will be maintained in the longer term, however, is an open question. This will depend on (*a*) the extent to which profitability figures in other industries remain relatively less attractive than in drugs; (*b*) the extent to which the downward pressure on prices exerted by the VPRS 'spills over' into export markets as foreign buyers use our domestic prices as their yardstick for negotiation and so further reduce pharmaceutical profitability; and (*c*) the continuance of managerial expectations that pharmaceutical R & D may still produce breakthroughs of major technical and commercial significance despite the evidence of the last decade that innovation is becoming both more rare and more costly.

3 State Participation in R & D

The Sainsbury Committee said:

> Nationalisation would have a strong tendency to lead to the central direction of research. We can see no reason why this should produce the best results; we doubt indeed whether it would be efficient. There may be an element of economic waste in competitive research but the evidence we have obtained leads us to believe that without such competition there would be a slower rate of discovery and innovation. This is not, in our view, the type of industry which would better serve the public interest under nationalisation.
>
> We therefore do not recommend nationalisation of this industry.[17]

Chapter 5 of the Opposition Green Paper on Health Care, however, gave as a reason why it advocated public ownership that there is '. . . neglect of possible lines of development which would help less common diseases . . .'[18]

Government subvention of R & D in an industry (by subsidy or actual performance) is generally justified on one or more of the following grounds:

1. the size of project requires more resources than the industrial unit has available;
2. project risks are too great for the industry to assume them; and
3. the market mechanism fails to reflect adequately the social benefits.

State aid to R & D, or its actual performance by a nationalised unit, cannot be justified on the first two grounds. There is no evidence that pharmaceutical R & D projects are of a size beyond the resource pool of many pharmaceutical firms. Most firms, in fact, conduct several projects simultaneously. Equally there is no supportive information to indicate that pharmaceutical firms are risk averters to the extent that R & D is not being conducted. With a one in 10,000 success rate, the evidence is rather pointing in the reverse direction.

The third category, however, is more likely to provide grounds for government support of industrial R & D in commercially unattractive disease areas, when the benefits recoupable through the market are less than the cost incurred, and both, in turn, are less than the social benefits. Clearly, in such circumstances a profit-maximising businessman will allocate his R & D effort towards the more common disease areas where the surplus of commercial benefits over costs is greatest.

This is clearly an attractive argument to those who see externalities lurking in every bargain made between a buyer and seller. The opportunity cost of such interference would, however, be far greater than any alleged benefits it might bring. Given a fixity in resources for pharmaceutical R & D then any increase in the research effort directed towards finding cures for less common diseases implies, of necessity, a reduction in R & D activity in the areas of higher disease incidence. (This is not an unrealistic assumption: the main R & D resource is trained manpower which is a fixed pool. An increase in the number of chemists, pharmacologists and the like cannot be obtained at a stroke.) Consequently government interference of the type suggested by the authors of the Green Paper might help the few, but it would harm the many.

9 Summary and Conclusions

1 Background

The preceding chapters have traced the development of the pharmaceutical industry from the days of the earliest primitive cures and 'quack' medicaments through to the present situation of a high-technology, multinational industry dependent on high levels of R & D and innovation for continued advance. Over the last forty years the industry has experienced dramatic and exciting growth. As a result of its achievements morbidity and mortality rates have dropped in a wide range of disease areas.

Table 9.1 Leading products and companies

Product (Rank order 1971, sterling sales)	*Company and Nationality of Innovator*	
1. Aldomet	Merck, Sharp & Dohme	USA
2. Valium	Roche	Switzerland
3. Penbritin	Beecham	UK
4. Lasix	Hoechst	Germany
5. Indocid	Merck, Sharpe & Dohme	USA
6. Intal	Fisons	UK
7. Ponderax	Servier	France
8. Librium	Roche	Switzerland
9. Betnovate	Glaxo	UK
10. Tofranil	Geigy	Switzerland
11. Inderal	ICI	UK
12. Brufen	Boots	UK
13. Synalar	Syntex	USA
14. Septrin	Wellcome	UK

Source: International Medical Statistics

Economically, pharmaceuticals is a growth sector of a growth industry, chemicals. Its market is the world and the sources of its growth, innovations, have international roots. Nationalistically the British industry has cause for pride. A report by the Centre for the Study of Industrial Innovation showed that in terms of cost efficiency the UK industry develops a new chemical entity at an average cost of only £1.6 million per compound. The comparative US cost is £4.0 million per compound.[1] Five of the leading fourteen drugs sold in Britain in 1971 were British discoveries (Table 9.1).

2 Market structure in the United Kingdom

Table 9.2 neatly summarises the pattern of market structure and so, implicitly, of competition in the industry.

No firm controls more than 9.2 per cent of the total market (company B is the largest company). All but the top three firms hold a

Table 9.2 Top twelve companies: number of products, main products' share of company sales and of sub-markets, 1969

Company	*No. of products*	*Main products*	*% of total company sales*	*% of sub-market**
A	49	1	39	37
		2	31	29
		3	10	33
		All others	20	
B	56	1	42	75
		2	28	51
		3	13	30
		All others	17	
C	75	1	49	49
		2	11	16
		All others	40	
D	36	1	76	45
		2	7	15
		All others	17	
E	37	1	36	29
		2	24	9
		3	19	43
		4	10	95
		All others	11	

Table 9.2 (cont.)

Company	*No. of products*	*Main products*	*% of total company sales*	*% of sub-market**
F	56	1	17	48
		2	16	25
		3	10	29
		All others	57	
G	11	1	85	56
		All others	15	
H	28	1	30	25
		2	30	20
		3	13	8
		All others	27	
I	71	1	25	7
		All others	75	
J	62	1	18	43
		2	17	7
		3	10	40
		All others	55	
K	45	1	21	8
		2	18	34
		3	13	19
		All others	48	

*It should be borne in mind that the concept of market definition depends upon the circumstances of the case. See, for example, the discussion on p. 122, *loc. cit.*

smaller than 5 per cent market share. Nevertheless at the level of the sub-market, industrial structure is not atomistic, but the reverse, highly concentrated.

Entry to the industry was shown to be common and continuing, albeit mainly springing from cross-entry activities from other nations or from other industries. Corporate decline was also shown to be a common feature. Many firms depend for the bulk of their turnover on relatively few products. Given relatively short product life-cycles successful R & D over time is essential to maintain corporate well-being. The three large US antibiotics firms who dominated the industry in the late 1950s and early 1960s are nowhere to be seen in Table 9.2.

Economic texts tend to concentrate on the theory of price competition. In reality firms compete with each other more by way of advertising and marketing activity, and by the 'test-tube' rivalry of new products. Nowhere is this more true than in pharmaceuticals. Inevitably, competing by product differentiation erects a barrier to entry with concomitant above 'normal' profits, obtrusive marketing, and R & D to obtain tangible product differences.

3 Profit levels

Pharmaceutical profit levels are high, but are volatile, unpredictable and are, on average, declining. Their absolute levels can be justified economically on the grounds of this unpredictability. Unless an above average return is present then investors will not provide capital where a high degree of risk is involved. This is supported by the evidence of large numbers of pharmaceutical firms diversifying out of the industry into fields where the rate of return is either perceived to be or is higher, or more certain.

This conclusion is not invalidated by the apparent paradox that some firms are not so diversifying or are indeed increasing their investment, through R & D, in the industry. Firstly, a few firms have had a continuous history of R & D successes and so have relatively high, if unfounded, confidence and expectation levels that the buffetings and vicissitudes of commercial and technological uncertainty will continue to pass them by. Secondly, despite declining profitability levels, relative to other industries, the pharmaceutical industry has maintained its position as a high profit investment location.

It would be imprudent to assume that this state of affairs will persist. Table 9.3 indicates that the dominant form of investment expenditure in pharmaceuticals is R & D. This is in sharp contrast to other industries. Moreover, R & D outlays have been more severely affected by rising cost pressures than have outlays for plant and equipment, which are the predominant form of investment by manufacturing industry generally.

This relatively great upward pressure on the cost of pharmaceutical investment (occasioned by increasing legislative complexity and a slow-down in the rate of discovery) coupled with continuing downward pressure on prices and profits by government buyers will, if unchecked, undoubtedly produce a situation where, at best, the industry will shift its R & D effort to more attractive national locations, and at worst into other industries.

Table 9.3 Ratio of R & D to plant and equipment outlays (six drug firms* compared with total US manufacturing)
Relative cost pressures on drug R & D and total US manufacturing investment on plant and equipment.

	Drug industry			*Total manufacturing*				
	R & D $m	*Plant & equipment $m*	*Ratio*	*R & D $m*	*Plant & equipment $m*	*Ratio*	*Drug R & D*	*Total manufacturing plant and equipment*
1961	92.1	53.4	1.7	4,605	14,330	0.3	100.0	100.0
1965	140.5	97.9	1.4	6,329	23,440	0.3	128.7	105.2
1969	224.0	167.7	1.3	9,660	31,680	0.3	166.2	120.5
1972	309.8	199.9	1.5	11,140	31,350	0.4	184.8	140.0

*Abbott, Lilly, Merck, Searle, S K & F, Upjohn.

Source: Economic Aspects of R & D Intensity in Pharmaceuticals (Washington: Jesse Friedman and Associates, 1973).

4 Product differentiation

Given the costliness of R & D it inevitably presents a barrier to entry to the industry to the smaller firm. Most R & D expenditure is directed at obtaining major advances. Most new products, however, are of fairly minor commercial and therapeutic significance. Minor advances in aggregate contribute to major steps forward; they can meet unfilled patient needs; they can provide rivalry to products which previously held monopoly situations; and they can provide firms with a continuing cash flow to hold together R & D teams during the lead times necessary to achieve major advances.

The suspicion remains that drug firms, because of their strategic interdependence in oligopolistic situations, will spend more on R & D than they or the market may need, in order to generate minor advances to maintain market position. This sort of minimax strategy may not be approved of either by prescribers or by firms, but there may be little either can do about it. Prescribers will continue to prescribe those few products in a therapeutic area which have clear-cut advantages. But they must, in so doing, provide for the R & D expenditure behind the plethora of other products with little turnover back-up of their own. Companies apparently continue to develop and launch such products, partly in the hope of improving market share and partly from fear that if they do not, others will introduce similar products, and they will lose market share. Except in the case of major products there is no evidence to support either of these hopes or fears. Nonetheless, so long as they are *perceived* to be real so long will firms be motivated to continue to develop a greater volume of minor products than could otherwise be justified.

It was suggested that, since *ex post* commercial experience has failed to alter such perceptions, then the *ex ante* knowledge that patent protection would vary according to whether or not an invention was a major or minor advance might result in greater selectivity in R & D performance.

The costs of such a system might be greater than the benefits it would provide. Most R & D is directed at discovering new chemical entities. Little is directed, in absolute terms, towards innovations with solely (real or imagined) competitive attractiveness even where such are patentable. A more serious barrier to entry was discovered in the area of promotion.

Here, companies were seen to promote more intensively than was necessary to provide the market size required for the financial support of innovative activity. However, it may be that this barrier to entry has been most overt only in the antibiotics sub-market; and that in the 1950s and early 1960s.

5 Legislative control

Even within the European Common Market a firm has to submit details of a new medicine to a safety committee in each of the nine countries if it wishes to sell it throughout the Community. Although these different committees share almost identical standards, an elaborate procedure with national variations must be repeated nine times. The EEC has expressed the desire to unify its rules or permit reciprocity but has not travelled far along the road of action.

The efficacy and safety of a drug can as a rule only be finally defined after it has been in widespread use for a number of years, perhaps even for a generation. If risks were to be excluded entirely there would be no alternative but to forbid the marketing of new drugs and to banish most of the existing ones.

To decide on the future direction of legislative control in the pharmaceutical industry one should ask two questions. First, who has the greatest volume of information and understanding of the conditions surrounding the supply and demand for medicines? Second, who has the most to lose if patient needs are not met in the most socially satisfactory manner? The answer to both questions is two-fold.

It is the members of the pharmaceutical market themselves who have the greatest volume of information about consumer needs and the means whereby they are met. It is the individual doctor who most intimately understands his own patient and who can best diagnose the ailment and the cure. It is the pharmaceutical firm, which after R & D lead times, often of over a decade, which most closely comprehends the chemical, pharmacological and clinical properties of its own products.

It is the individual doctor and his patient who have the greatest incentive to demand the most appropriate product. It is the pharmaceutical firm which has the greatest incentive to ensure that such products are available when patient needs, and so prescriptions and consequently profits, are present.

In other words it is the members of the pharmaceutical market themselves who know best when and what decisions have to be made about prescription choice, R & D project selection and market innovation. It is the members of the pharmaceutical market themselves who have most to lose from faulty decisions and who therefore have the greatest incentive to take correct decisions relating to the production and consumption of medicines.

The doctor who prescribes a sub-optimal medicine for a given disease will find that his waiting-room clears less quickly than that of his colleague who has made a more accurate diagnosis and so choice of therapeutic agent. The pharmaceutical firm which fails to market products which are satisfactory in terms of comparative efficacy, absorption, toxicity or whatever will fail to have its products prescribed and so lose profits. There is certainly a loss to society involved if either the drug firm or the doctor make wrong decisions. But the loss is borne by the firm through lower earnings and/or by the doctor and patient as a result of the prescription of a sub-optimal medicine.*

In such circumstances is it likely that legislators, however benevolent and well-meaning, will take decisions, which from the viewpoint of the patient, will be as satisfactory as those taken by the members of the pharmaceutical market itself? They neither have as high a degree of knowledge, nor do they have the incentive to know what firms, doctors and patients desire in their own best interests.

Their product knowledge will be limited to written reports and restricted tests which cannot compare with the intimate knowledge of the R & D workers and clinicians who have worked closely on a product over a span of years. Their patient knowledge will be restricted to sociological surveys which will highlight means, medians and sub-groups but which will not indicate the scope for 'detail in prescribing' which is the strength of the GP system in meeting the varying needs, especially over time, of the individual patient.

Not only do legislators not 'know best', they lack the incentive to make the right decision, as they have less to lose if the make the wrong one. A doctor making a wrong decision may see his patient die or at least deteriorate. A pharmaceutical firm making a wrong decision will at best suffer a loss of immediate profits, and at worst lose its reputation as a responsible company and so potentially lose its very existence.

In fact, the incentive to the legislators may not only be less but be reversed. Both industrial managers and civil servants are motivated by the prospects of career advancement and of power. In the case of the

*This ignores the losses to the government in the form of lower corporation tax receipts, any monopoly distortions associated with product differentiation or promotion decisions.

manager, his goal is achieved if he meets the needs of the consumer, and this is reflected by increased profits. In the case of the legislator there is no such yardstick. The measure of success now becomes volume and detail of work. Unfortunately there may well be a negative correlation between such bureaucracy and the meeting of consumer need. (See, for example, Table 8.2 and its associated discussion.)*

6 Where the future may lead

The Labour Party Green Paper was 'worried about whether drug firms can attract the most able and imaginative scientists into their service. A system which allowed much greater contact . . . with the Universities would offer many advantages'.[2] This statement is at odds both with the industry's history of achievement and with the cordial relationships which exist between drug firms and the academic environment.

In a sense, however, the authors of the Green Paper, perhaps unwittingly, have put their finger on one of the weakest links in the chain which stretches from basic disease knowledge to a marketable human medicament. The basic researchers working in the universities have *not* delivered. The raw material of knowledge necessary for efficient applied research at the level of the firm is largely unavailable. In Chapter 7 we saw that there was no such phenomenon as 'medical orthodoxy'. Schools of thought, usually at variance with each other, exist and vary over time. 'Good medical practice' varies in interpretation from practitioner to practitioner. In Chapter 4 we saw that most pharmaceutical R & D is random, not systematic, in nature. This results in trial-and-error management control rather than the use of specifically pre-programmed techniques. Numerate and effective R & D project selection techniques are rarely used by firms in the early stages of a project's life.[3] In an industry like pharmaceuticals, where management methods are otherwise highly sophisticated, this is unexpected.

Jantsch has argued that project selection (or technological forecasting) attempts to answer four basic questions:

1. The time span required (for a project's completion).
2. The effort required (for the project's completion).
3. The market impact (of the project's completion).

*The economic theory of bureaux is discussed in *Bureaucracy: Servant or Master?* W. A. Niskanen. Institute of Economic Affairs, 1973.

4. The selection of a suitable technological starting point, from where to commence the R & D required to arrive at the specified project goal (namely the setting out of terms of reference for the project indicating from where and how the goal will be achieved).

The answer to this last question Jantsch refers to as a characteristic of 'normative' forecasting. In the pharmaceutical industry there is an '*enforced absence of normative forecasting*' because of the poorly developed technological base on which the industry rests. R & D is random rather than rational. Random R & D, by definition, does not select a specific starting point, or if it does then the project goal will be hazy and non-specified. If one or other, or sometimes both, of two ends of the R & D continuum is ill-defined and uncertain then it is impossible to get a yardstick, of whatever complexity, to measure the distance (i.e. the cost) from an unknown technological starting point to an unknown or ill-defined goal or end-point.

There may, therefore, be an 'enforced absence' of numerate project selection techniques in the drug industry. The long-term solution to this is to increase the performance of basic research, into, for example, the sciences of molecular biology and to increase understanding of the actions of chemicals in the body. Such understanding would open up possibilities of action prediction. This would provide both the starting point, a specific although hitherto unsynthesised chemical with a predicted action, and the goal, the impact of that action on a specific disease. The 'distance' between the two could then be measured by some appropriate yardstick or technique and the projects with the shortest 'distances', or some other measured attractions, would be chosen for priority development.

The deliberate concentration on in-house fundamental research into molecular biology by firms such as Pfizer corroborate the view that there is a short fall in the supply of information at this level. Scientific advance, then, would improve corporate decision taking at the level of project selection, cheapen R & D procedures, and facilitate product choice by prescribers.

When this scientific advance does take place the benefits could be immense. Instead of synthesising 5000 chemicals to obtain one marketable medicine, one synthesis might suffice. The risks and the expense of clinical trials will be reduced. The prescriber will at last have a generally accepted yardstick of efficacy. And the scope for subjective disagreements and the resource misallocation which can result from sub-optimal prescribing patterns will at last be minimised.

> Who shall decide when doctors disagree
> And soundest casuists doubt, like you and me?
>
> Alexander Pope

References

Chapter 1

1. G. E. Trease, *Pharmacy in History* (London, 1964), p. 235.
2. R. Calder, *The Lifer Savers* (Pan, 1961), p. 20.
3. For a fuller and more informative discussion on the story behind modern pharmaceuticals, L. G. Matthews, *A History of Pharmacy in Britain* (Edinburgh, 1962), is recommended.
4. H. M. Bottcher, *Miracle Drugs* (Heinemann, 1959), p. 190.
5. B. A. Weisbrod, *Economics of Public Health* (University of Pennsylvania Press, 1961), pp. 30–1.
6. Information provided by the Association of the British Pharmaceutical Industry (ABPI).
7. Department of Health and Social Security, *Annual Reports* 1957, 1967 and 1972.
8. S. Taylor, *Good General Practice* (1954).
9. Dr A. I. Richardson, *Guardian*, 14 March 1964.

Chapter 2

1. P. S. Mould, 'The Pharmaceutical Industry and the Balance of Payments', in G. Teeling-Smith (ed.), *The Pharmaceutical Industry and Society* (Office of Health Economics, 1972), p. 48.
2. E. Penrose, *The Theory of the Growth of the Firm* (Blackwell, 1958), Chapter VII.
3. *Annual Report*, Chas. Pfizer Inc. (New York, 1964).
4. *Annual Report*, Chas. Pfizer Inc. (New York, 1966).
5. Syntex Corporation, *A Corporation and a Molecule*, p. 95.
6. *Annual Report*, Syntex Corporation (1967).
7. *A Corporation and a Molecule*, op. cit., p. 83.
8. *Annual Report*, Eli Lilly Corporation (1960).

Chapter 3

1. *Report of the Committee of Inquiry into the Relationship of the Pharmaceutical Industry with the National Health Service* (Sainsbury Report) (Cmnd 3140, HMSO, 1967), p. 102.
2. M. H. Cooper, *Prices and Profits in the Pharmaceutical Industry* (Pergamon, 1966), p. 244.
3. *MIMS*, April 1966.
4. *Sunday Times Business News*, 18 August 1968.
5. ABPI information.
6. Cooper, op. cit., p. 62.
7. Penrose, op. cit., p. 142.
8. W. D. Reekie, 'Barriers to Entry and Competition' in G. Teeling-Smith (ed.), *Economics and Innovation in the Pharmaceutical Industry* (OHE, 1970).
9. *British Rate and Data* (1968).

Chapter 4

1. K. G. Smith, 'Profitability and R and D' in G. Teeling-Smith (ed.), *The Pharmaceutical Industry and Society* (OHE, 1972).
2. OECD estimate, *Gaps in Technology – Pharmaceuticals* (OECD, 1969).
3. ABPI information.
4. J. Y. Bogue, 'Organisation and Economics of Research in the Pharmaceutical Industry', *Pharmaceutical Journal* (1962).
5. J. T. Litchfield, 'Evaluation of Drugs in Experimental Animals', in P. Talalay (ed.), *Drugs in Our Society* (Johns Hopkins University Press, 1960).
6. Sainsbury, op. cit., p. 61.
7. Opposition Green Paper, *Health Care* (Labour Party, 1973), p. 41.
8. Sainsbury, op. cit., p. 55.
9. D. R. Laurence, *Clinical Pharmacology* (London, 1960), p. 87.
10. Calder, op. cit., p. 59.
11. U. S. House of Representatives, *Hearings before the Anti-Trust and Monopoly Sub-Committee, 1961–62.*
12. W. S. Comanor, 'Research and Competitive Product Differentiation in the Pharmaceutical Industry in the United States', *Economica* (1964).

13. Cooper, op. cit., p. 41.
14. OECD, op. cit., p. 23.
15. Ibid., p. 17.

Chapter 5

1. R. Harris and A. Seldon, *Advertising and the Public* (Deutsch, 1962), p. 75.
2. R Bauer and M. Field, 'Ironic Contrast: U.S. and U.S.S.R. Drug Industries', *Harvard Business Review* (1962).
3. Sainsbury, op. cit., p. 68.
4. E. Whitehead, *District Nursing* (1964), (emphasis added).
5. E. Kefauver, *In A Few Hands* (Pelican, 1964), p. 77.
6. Sainsbury, op. cit., p. 65.
7. ABPI Survey.
8. ABPI, *Annual Reports.*
9. Sainsbury, op. cit., p. 151.
10. Ibid., p. 102.
11. Cooper, op. cit., p. 94.
12. PAC, *Minutes of Evidence*, 1964–65, Class 6, Vote 8, Appendix V.
13. *British Medical Journal*, 30 March 1968.
14. A. W. Beckett, 'The Cost of Safety in Medicines', in G. Teeling-Smith (ed.), *The Pharmaceutical Industry and Society* (OHE, 1972).
15. Sainsbury, op. cit., p. 78.
16. W. Duncan Reekie, 'Some Problems Associated with the Marketing of Ethical Pharmaceutical Products', *Journal of Industrial Economics* (1970).
17. W. Taplin, 'Advertising Appropriation Policies', *Economica.*
18. B. Inglis, *Drugs, Doctors and Diseases* (Mayflower, 1962), p. 13.

Chapter 6

1. E. A. G. Robinson, *Monopoly* (Cambridge, 1938), p. 120.
2. Inglis, op. cit., p. 206.
3. Ibid., p. 33.
4. Cooper, op. cit., p. 159.
5. *The British Patent System* (Cmnd 4407, HMSO, 1970) (Banks Committee Report).

6. K. Boehm and A. Silberston, *The British Patent System* (Cambridge, 1967).
7. Fuller lists relating to each Section are provided in Boehm, op. cit., pp. 102–10.
8. *The Economist*, 6 January 1968.
9. Boehm, op. cit., p. 108.
10. H. Steele, 'Monopoly and Competition in the Ethical Drug Market', *Journal of Law and Economics* (1962).
11. J. W. Markham, 'Inventive Activity: Government Controls and the Legal Environment', in R. R. Nelson (ed.), *The Rate and Direction of Inventive Activity* (Princeton, 1962), p. 602.

Chapter 7

1. *The Cost of the National Health Service in England and Wales* (HMSO, 1956) (Guillebaud).
2. *Final Report of the Committee on the Cost of Prescribing* (HMSO, 1959) (Hinchcliffe).
3 Ibid., p. 27.
4. *The Times*, 3 February 1961.
5. 'Administered Prices: Drugs', US Senate Sub-Committee on Anti-Trust, 1961 (Kefauver).
6. Kefauver, op. cit., p. 34.
7. Sainsbury, op. cit., p. 53.
8. Department of Health, *Annual Report, 1972*, p. 12.
9. ABPI, *Annual Report, 1967*, p. 7.
10. *Prescriber's Journal*, April 1968, p. 8.
11. Ibid., p. 11.
12. *The Economist*, 5 July 1969, p. 20.
13. Inglis, op. cit., p. 186.
14. E. H. Chamberlain, 'Product Heterogeneity and Public Policy', *American Economic Review* (1950).
15. L. R. Oliker, 'The Pharmaceutical Industry: Statutory Review', (unpublished doctoral thesis, Indiana University, 1967).
16. G. Wyndham-Davies, *The Pharmaceutical Industry* (Pergamon), p. 67.
17. Cited in Wyndham-Davies, op. cit., p. 98.
18. Laurence, op. cit., pp. 4 and 5.
19. *The Economist*, 6 January 1973.

Chapter 8

1. J. Schumpeter, *Capitalism, Socialism and Democracy* (Harrap, 1950).
2. The Monopolies Commision, *Beecham Group Ltd and Glaxo Group Ltd: The Boots Co. Ltd and Glaxo Group Ltd: A Report on the Proposed Mergers* (H.C.341, 1972), pp. 49–51.
3. J. Jewkes, D. Sawers and R. Stillerman, *The Sources of Invention* (2nd ed., Macmillan, 1970).
4. G. H. Grabowski, 'The Determinants of Industrial Research and Development: A Study of the Chemical, Drug and Petroleum Industries', *Journal of Political Economy* (1968).
5. E. Mansfield, *Industrial Research and Technological Innovation* (Norton, 1968).
6. Monopolies Commission, op. cit., p. 68.
7. W. Duncan Reekie, 'Location and Relative Efficiency of Research and Development in the Pharmaceutical Industry', *Business Ratios* (1969).
8. David Schwartzman, 'Research Activity and Size of Firm in the US Pharmaceutical Industry' (mimeographed, New School for Social Research, New York, 1973).
9. William S. Comanor, 'Research and Technical Change in the Pharmaceutical Industry', *Review of Economics and Statistics* (1965).
10. A. Angilley, 'Returns to Scale in Research in the Ethical Pharmaceutical Industry: Some Further Empirical Evidence', *Journal of Industrial Economics* (1973).
11. E. Mansfield, J. Rapaort, J. Schee, S. Wagner and M. Hamburger, *Research and Innovation in the Modern Corporation* (Norton, 1971).
12. Sainsbury, op. cit., p. 41.
13. The Monopolies Commission, *Chlordiazepoxide and Diazepam* (H.C. 197, 1973), para. 218.
14. Ibid., para. 235.
15. G. Polanyi, *Which Way Monopoly Policy?* (IEA Research Monograph, no. 30, 1973), p. 46.
16. Ibid. pp. 52–3.
17. Sainsbury, op. cit.
18. Green Paper, op. cit., p. 41.

Chapter 9

1. Centre for the Study of Industrial Innovation, *Innovative Activity in the Pharmaceutical Industry* (NEDO, 1973).
2. Green Paper, op. cit., p. 41.
3. NEDO, op. cit., p. 45.
4. E. Jantsch, *Technological Forecasting in Perspective* (OECD, Paris, 1967), p. 27.
5. Ibid., p. 56.

Index